Going Straight

A play

Richard Harris

Samuel French — London
www.samuelfrench-london.co.uk

GOING STRAIGHT

First produced by Bill Kenwright at the Theatre Royal, Windsor, on 3rd September 2004, with the following cast:

Michael	John Alderton
Brenda	Pauline Collins
Ray	George Costigan
Francine	Carol Royle
Polly	Kate Alderton

Directed by Alan Strachan
Designed by Hayden Griffin

CHARACTERS

Michael, mid-sixties
Brenda, early sixties
Ray, mid-sixties
Francine, early forties
Polly, late twenties

Man, voice only, Spanish

SYNOPSIS OF SCENES

The action of the play takes place in the main sitting-room of Michael's and Francine's villa in Southern Spain

ACT I   September. Early afternoon
ACT II   Later that evening

Time — the present

AUTHOR'S NOTE

I'm aware that purpose-made CCTV recordings may well be outside the financial range of some groups or companies considering performing this play. I would therefore suggest that a tape recorder could be used instead. In fact, it was tape recorder in my first draft and it was John Alderton who came up with the much more theatrical idea of using visual recording rather than just sound and Bill Kenwright who was willing to provide the necessary. But, as I say, a tape recorder, the playback suitably edited and magnified, would be perfectly acceptable. Certain sections of the play would of course need to be either cut or re-written and I would be more than happy to provide my version for those who might be interested.

I'm also aware that there is a considerable amount of "bad language" used in the play. It is not gratuitous, it is inevitable with characters such as Michael and Raymond and to cut out the swearing would, apart from anything else, destroy much of the rhythm of their speech. Raymond's long speech near the end of Act One is a good example of this and you will notice how he and Michael moderate their language in the presence of ladies. Whether we like it or not, the F-word nowadays seems as acceptable as "bloody" which, in my youth, got you a clip round the ear. It is the C-word that remains largely unacceptable and it has been suggested that in this play it could be replaced by the word "prick". (No doubt someone can tell us why the P-word is okay but the C-word isn't). So much as I would like the play to be performed as written I can see the problem and the need for you to moderate some - but please, not all - of the "bad language" as you feel necessary.

R.H.

FOR DAVID

Other plays published by Richard Harris
published by Samuel French Ltd

Albert
The Business of Murder
Dead Guilty
A Foot in the Door
Ghosts (adapted from J Basil Cowlishaw's translation
of the play by Henrik Ibsen)
In Two Minds
Is It Something I Said?
Local Affairs
The Maintenance Man
Outside Edge
Party Piece
Stepping Out
Stepping Out — The Musical
(with lyrics by Mary Stewart-David
and music by Denis King)
Visiting Hour

ACT I

Early afternoon. September. The tastefully-styled main sitting-room of a large villa in Southern Spain

US there is a raised area that includes a bar. A large flat television screen is set into the US wall. At the moment it is concealed. At the rear, glazed doors open on to a terrace that leads to a large and secluded garden. Arches give access to other areas of the house, including a kitchen, L. DL an alcove gives on to the unseen main door and a cloakroom. A wide staircase, L, leads to the upper floor. The furniture on the main, lower, level includes a reclining swivel chair with matching footstool

When the play begins, Ray sits looking at a silver-framed photograph. He is in his mid-sixties, pale-skinned, wearing an unstylish lightweight suit and tie. Michael stands behind him, glass of beer in hand, looking down proudly at the photograph. He too is in his mid-sixties, fit, lightly tanned, wearing a stylish casual shirt and trousers and a Rolex watch

And we go straight in, with:

Michael Am I right or am I right?
Ray No question.
Michael Four years old last Monday.
Ray She's beautiful.
Michael A little princess.
Ray Beautiful.
Michael I could, I could eat her.
Ray Image of your Cheryl.
Michael Not much.
Ray Image she is — look at the eyes.
Michael And the things she comes out with.
Ray Like I say, like your Cheryl.

Ray returns the photograph to Michael who remains looking at it fondly as:

Michael You know what she said? Last time I had my little chat with her?

Ray What's that?

Michael We always have this little chat on the phone — every week.

Ray Nice.

Michael Grandad she says ... you know Jesus? Yes sweetheart I says — what about Jesus? Well she says ... is he really the son of God?

Ray Break your heart, don't they?

Michael Well my little sweetheart I says ... some people think he is and some people think he isn't.

Ray I know what you mean — tricky.

Michael And you know what she says? Four years old. You know what she says?

Ray Tell me.

Michael She says ... well ... if some people think he is and some people think he isn't ... why can't he have a DNA test?

Ray That is, that is beautiful.

Michael I mean is that or is that not special?

Ray Beautiful.

Michael Four years old. (*He has returned the photograph to its place amongst others*)

Ray Kids today though, eh Mickey? The things they come out with.

Michael D'you know what I think? I think it's all these computers.

Ray Don't talk to me about computers.

Michael That one I got in the office — (*he vaguely indicates*) — two grand.

Ray Yeah?

Michael Francine. You've got to have the best.

Ray State of the art.

Michael State of the fucking art — sweetheart I said, when it comes to computers state of the art lasts about five fucking minutes — you switch it *on* and it's outa date.

Ray I've stuck with the one I've had from the beginning.

Michael It does everything — everything. Well it would do if I could understand the fucking thing.

Ray I had a few lessons — just the basics — you know — enough to do the writing, emails, the wassit — the web ...

Michael Course, you've gotta waddayacallit ...

Ray Website.

Michael Look at this, Francine said. Your friend Raymond's got his own website.

Ray Yeah well, they expect it.

Michael Makes you a few bob, does it?

Ray A few bob, yeah ...

Michael *You* take it while it's going, my son.

Ray Exactly.

Michael I mean it's business, innit? What we might call your little … (*fluttering a hand*) cottage industry.

Ray Yeah. Right.

Michael Whoda thought though, eh Raymondo?

Ray Yeah

Michael Fifty years ago, whoda thought?

Ray Yeah.

Michael Coupla kids on the make — and *now*…

Ray Yeah. Yeah.

They dwell on it for a moment and:

Michael Fifty years. Is that how long it is?

Ray More like sixty as it happens.

Michael Sixty fucking years. Unbe-fuckin-lievable.

Again they dwell on the thought. Ray pulls out a packet of cigarettes and makes to take one out but:

Michael Sorry Ray, d'you mind? Francine's got a thing about it, won't have 'em in the house.

Ray Right.

Michael Specially not in the bedrooms.

Ray Right.

Michael I mean me, you could catch fire as far as I'm concerned — but — you know — sorry mate.

Ray No no it's — OK, Brenda don't like me doing it anyway. Well I'm supposed to stop — you know. (*He pats his chest*)

Michael Finding it hard, are you?

Ray Terrible.

Michael I know I know. Listen. If you're really desperate there's a little place down the end of the garden where we keep the tools and stuff.

Ray (*grinning*) Right.

Michael Don't just stub 'em out though: there's a little pot round the back.

Ray That what *you* do?

Michael I must admit to the odd cigar. Not that er … (*He touches the side of his nose*)

Ray Not a word — and same with Bren, OK?

Michael Absolutely.

This moment. Two naughty boys

So … when it comes to computers — I dabble — and that's about it.

Ray That's a good word — dabble.

Michael But kids? Like they was born to it.

Ray Another world innit?

Michael Not much.

Ray Their world, Mickey, the likes of you and me are dinosaurs.

Michael Oh that's fucking charming, that is.

Ray No no — in *their* eyes.

Michael That what you got on your website is it? www dinosaur?

Ray It's what that wassisname called us, didn't he?

Michael What wassisname?

Ray Wassisname — that writer bloke — he had that book out last month.

Michael Not *him*.

Ray Him, yeah — what did you think of it?

Michael Think of what?

Ray His book.

Michael I'm with Hitler, mate, I'd burn his fucking book.

Ray You have read it though.

Michael Course I haven't fucking read it.

Ray Thought you read 'em all.

Michael Don't tell me *you* read his fucking rubbish.

Ray Just — you know — skipped through it.

Michael Who is he anyway? Some pouf who shaves his head and gets his thrills playing footsie with the bad boys.

Ray Lot of 'em about, Mickey.

Michael Fucking hangers-on. Read his book? Bollocks, I wouldn't give him the fucking pleasure. What does *he* know anyway? What do any of 'em know?

Ray What we tell 'em.

Michael You're right. What we tell 'em.

Ray And the man is after all only making a living.

Michael No, you're right. Course you're right. You cannot blame a man for making a living. Even if it's off someone else's back and even if he's a lying bastard of the first order.

Was there a double edge on this? They dwell on it for a moment and:

What started all that off?

Ray Er ... computers. Kids and computers.

Michael Yeah — well — computers or no computers, they're your kids, you love 'em.

Ray Family. It's a strong thing.

Michael And I'll tell you something else — never thought I'd say it, never thought I'd say it ——
Ray Being a grandad.
Michael Being a grandad.
Ray My lot tear my heart out.
Michael I used to think — "Grandad? Leave it out."
Ray Tell me about it.
Michael But now ——
Ray I know what you mean, I know exactly what you mean.
Michael "Can you help me, Grandad?" "'Course I can help you, my little darling" … I love it, I do I love it.
Ray Yeah.
Michael Love it.
Ray See much of 'em, do you?
Michael Oh yeah. They was over at Easter.
Ray Lovely for a young family though, eh, Mickey? The pool and everything.
Michael "Next time you come over, Grandad's gonna teach you to swim," I said.
Ray And you will.
Michael Too fucking right I will. Little Lisa — not Jason, he swims like fucking Jaws.

An electronic buzzer sounds. Michael looks towards it, not expecting anyone. Then moves to take up the intercom telephone that is mounted on the wall next to an unseen VDU near the main door

Yes?
Man (*voice-over*) *Tengo las plantas.*
Michael *Mueve — no te veo. OK OK — que plantas?*
Man (*voice-over*) *Para la senora Kavanagh.*

Michael considers for a moment and:

Michael *Momento.* (*He presses another button, waits a moment — his eyes never leaving the VDU — and, into the phone*) It's me, babe. Did you order some plants for the garden? ... Yeah, he's here now. ... Right, yeah, OK. (*He presses another button and:*) *Vale, entra. Asegurate que la puerta esta cerrada.* (*He presses the entry button, puts down the phone but remains looking at the screen, as:*)
Ray Good you speaking the old lingo though, eh Mickey?
Michael I went to classes. Francine insisted. She's right, it shows respect. I said make sure it's shut, arsehole. Thank you. (*He moves away*) Bloke with some stuff for the garden.

Ray You have to be well-careful I imagine.

Michael (*his mind on the unseen man*) What's that?

Ray Security. Place like this. Geezer with *your* form, you never know *who* might come knocking, eh Mickey?

The last bit said lightly but:

Michael That supposed to be funny is it Raymond?

Ray No, I just meant...

Michael I know what you meant and I don't think it's very funny and I don't want you repeating it in front of Francine.

Ray Fucking hell Mickey I was just — fucking hell ...

It's a tricky little moment, but:

Michael You get a lot of unnecessaries ... gypsies when we first come here, now it's so-called political refugees looking to put their hand in your pocket — I'll cut the bleeding thing off sunshine I said to the last one who showed his face here.

Ray Same wherever you go nowadays. Half the world on the move and the other half getting shoved up into a corner.

Michael has moved to stand looking out over the terrace

Michael There's also a lotta straight thieving goes on. Local kids. I think they do it as an O level.

Ray Francine said you had to get rid of the couple who was looking after you.

Michael That's what I mean. You treat 'em like royalty and then find out they've been thieving the eyes off you. (*Calling*) *Necesitas algo de mi?*

Man (*off*) *No te preocupes, sigo el mio.*

Michael *Gracias.* (*Under his breath*) Cunt. (*He drinks his beer and indicates*) How you doing with the water?

Ray Good. (*He takes a sip*)

Michael You're sure you wouldn't fancy a beer — a glass of wine — juice — we've got some beautiful fresh orange juice.

Ray Not for me, Mickey, thanks.

Throughout the following, Michael will keep half an eye on what is going on, unseen, outside

Michael Your stomach still playing up?

Ray I get gas — you know.
Michael When didn't you get gas?
Ray Gas is my cross.
Michael Still on them Rennies, are you?
Ray I gotta prescription.
Michael You and them bleedin' Rennies.
Ray Yeah.
Michael I remember saying to Dave — that first big job we done — that wholesalers — what's he up to now, I says, he's wearing lipstick, he's wearing white bloody lipstick — no no Mickey he says, that's not lipstick that's all this chalk stuff he chews. Thank Gawd for that I says, I thought he was turning into one of these stringvestites.
Ray Leave it out, Mick.
Michael I'm telling you.
Ray Leave it out.

They dwell lightly on the thought and:

Ray It was a garridge.
Michael What?
Ray That first big job we done.
Michael It was that wholesalers, that *schmutter* place.
Ray No it was that garridge on Newport Street. Friday dinner time, we done the wages.

It looks as though Michael will argue but:

Michael You're right. You're fucking right. Fuck me. (*He frowns, concerned at his capricious memory but just as soon:*) Watch the fucking flowers!
Man (*off*) *Como?*
Michael *Ten cuidado las flores,* you cunt.
Man (*off*) Is OK.
Michael No it isn't fucking okay — *ten cuidado.* What are they doing up there?
Ray Woman's perjorative, innit? They try something on, then they try something else on, then when they're happy they take it all off and go to the toilet.
Michael We'll have a look, shall we?
Ray Eh?

Michael has taken up the TV remote control from the footstool. He activates it and the television is revealed and shows split-screen images of all the rooms in the house

Ray What's all this?

Michael Part of my fifty grand security system. I can sit here and survey my entire kingdom. Swimming pool ... garden ... Old Kent Road ... now then ... the George Walker suite ...

Ray Leave it out, she might be doing something personal.

Michael I'm kidding, I'm kidding. (*He grins, switches off the screen and tosses down the remote control*) Listen — about Cheryl. Don't mention her in front of Francine. She gets a bit umpty, people talking about Cheryl all the time.

Ray Understandable.

Michael Just — you know — use your noddle.

Ray Course I will. She's a lovely woman, Mickey, your Francine.

Michael I knew you'd like her. You especially.

Ray Yeah?

Michael She knows all about *you*, y'know.

Ray Yeah?

Michael You and me.

Ray Yeah?

Michael I said to her: we go back, Raymond and me.

Ray We do.

Michael I mean really back.

Ray The odd scrape or two, eh Mickey?

Michael Wine, women and mind your own fucking business.

Ray Yeah, we was naughty all right. You the naughtiest of all.

Michael Down the chemist of a Friday night ... three packets of Durex please and six packets of Rennies for my friend here.

Ray And the rest.

Michael How did we do it, eh? Eh?

Ray That age, you do, dontcha?

Michael You do, mate, you fucking do. Now look at us.

Ray You look great.

Michael I still do a bit. You know. Fifty lengths a day, down the gym maybe once or twice a week.

Ray And the hair, you've still got all your hair, you lucky bastard.

Michael Baby Bio and plenty of sunshine.

Ray You and your hair — where's Mickey they'd say, tooling up? No I'd say, arranging his fucking barnet.

They enjoy the memory and:

Michael I let myself go right down, you know. After Cheryl went, God rest her. Blamed myself. You know. Bringing her out here. Wondering if she'd still be alive if we'd stayed where we was. All that bollocks. Then I met Francine and ... well. She's my angel.

Ray nods. If there's something he wants to say, he's not going to. Instead, he stands and moves to look out over the terrace. This moment and:

Michael Listen. About the wedding. It was a cockup, all right?

Ray You don't have to ...

Michael I want to tell you, I want to tell you ... we cocked up the invitations, you shoulda been invited and somehow you wasn't, it's as simple as that.

Ray I know that, Mickey, course I know that.

Michael It was only a little affair — you know — mostly family.

Ray Forget it, Mickey.

Michael Jesus Christ I said, how could this happen, he's my oldest friend.

Ray It doesn't matter.

Michael It does fucking matter.

Ray I'm here now inn I?

Michael As long as there's no ill-feeling.

Ray Mickey.

Michael Swear to me there's no ill-feeling

Ray I don't have to swear to you — you *know*.

Michael Because — you know.

Ray I swear — there's no ill-feeling. There never was, there never will be.

This moment

Michael Anyway. It's good to see you.

Ray Yeah.

Michael We left it too long. Why did we leave it so long? (*He puts his arms around Ray*)

After a brief moment, Ray responds but with much more naked emotion

> *They are in this embrace when Brenda comes in from upstairs. She's in her early sixties but still with much evidence of the natural looker she once was. Her new holiday outfit isn't quite right. High heels. Her tan is a little too golden, a little too even. She's shoving stuff into a small bag and, seeing the two men:*

Brenda I wouldn't bank on the earth moving, he's got prostrate trouble.

Michael (*breaking away*) Hallo Brenda, love.

Ray All right sweetheart?

Brenda There's someone in your garden.

Michael Yeah, he's delivering some plants — how's your room?
Brenda Beautiful,
Michael Do you, will it?
Brenda It's lovely. (*Of her necklace*)   Take this off for me, will you
   Ray, it's got stuck again.
Michael Allow me.
Brenda Ray can do it, thank you.

*Behind her back, Michael grins, raising eyebrows at Ray who takes off
the necklace as:*

Michael How about that view?
Brenda Beautiful. (*To Ray*) I didn't pack the insect repellent.
Michael You won't need insect repellent.
Brenda You always get stung, you know you do.
Michael You need some, we've got some.
Brenda We go to the pictures and he gets stung.
Ray There y'go.

Ray gives Brenda the necklace which she will put into her bag as:

Brenda Four o'clock on a November afternoon in Palmers Green, how
   does he get stung? (*She gives him a brief but fond kiss on the cheek*)
Ray I didn't get stung, I said I *thought* I'd got stung.
Brenda You had a lump come up.
Ray It wasn't a lump, it was a whatsit.
Brenda It was a lump — the woman in the next seat had to climb over
   it.
Ray Sit down, Bren, there's a good girl.
Brenda I've been sitting down all morning. (*Nevertheless, she sits*)

*During the above, Michael has moved to stand looking out across the
terrace*

Michael I'll tell you this: sitting or standing, you're still as beautiful
   as ever.
Brenda And you're still full of you-know-what.
Michael She must have a secret — what's your secret, Bren?
Brenda Embalming fluid.
Michael Well, whatever it is it gives you a great tan.
Ray (*quickly*) We're not long back from Florida.

*Francine enters from upstairs. She is in her early forties. Good-
looking, classy, beautifully-dressed, carrying a large sunhat. And not
a trace of a tan*

Francine (*with a gracious smile*) Sorry to keep you — I've been trying to phone the wretched bank.

Michael No luck?

Francine Well I finally got through but Alvarez wasn't "available" of course.

Michael Well that's it then, babe: you'll have to go and play the *memsahib* as per.

Francine Did I hear someone mention Florida?

Michael Ray and Bren have just come back from there.

Francine D'you know, I've never been to Florida.

Michael I was saying what a great tan she's got …

Man (*calling, off*) Señor.

Michael *Vale, vale, vengo* — he'll be wanting his money.

Michael goes on to the terrace and out of sight

Francine will take up a small pad and make notes of things she needs to do in town, as:

Francine I didn't know it was that hot at this time of year.

Ray Sorry?

Francine Florida.

Brenda It was where *we* went.

Francine It doesn't worry you then, Brenda?

Brenda What's that, Francine?

Francine The sun.

Brenda Not really, no.

Francine I must say I avoid it like mad. We both do. Michael not as much as he should, perhaps, but I'm getting him there.

Ray Mad dogs and West Ham supporters, eh?

Francine (*writing, and so, "absently"*) Apart from the health thing, a dried-up skin can look so unbecoming, don't you think? Especially on the not-so-young. (*She finishes writing*) Although I must say that your skin looks lovely, Brenda. Just the right shade.

Ray She uses a lot of moisturiser, don't you Brenda?

Brenda As it happens, it's not a sun tan — all my liver spots have joined up.

Michael appears

Michael Come and sort this out, will you, babe, I think he's trying to stitch us up.

Francine I shouldn't think he is for two minutes.

Michael Well whatever, I need you to sort it.

Michael gives Francine a flat smile and goes out of sight

Francine I've got to go and do my interpreter bit — Michael tries bless him but he's still very limited — do excuse me.

Francine goes through to the terrace and out of sight, putting on her hat as she does so

Brenda "I didn't know it was that hot at this time of year". Condescending cow. She knows perfectly well it's out of a bottle.
Ray We could have just said we haven't had a holiday, you know, Brenda love.
Brenda I don't want him thinking he's giving us another handout.
Ray It isn't like that.
Brenda Two years you don't hear a word from him and suddenly we get the royal invitation.
Ray Sweetheart, sweetheart — why do you have to be so suspicious all the time?
Brenda Because I have to do it for the pair of us.
Ray (*choosing to change the subject*) Well I'll tell you this: bottle or not you look terrific.
Brenda Oh yeah — there's her walking about like Mary Bleedin' Poppins and there's me looking like Dale Bloody Winton.
Ray She's all right.
Brenda She's a cow.
Ray Give her a break.
Brenda "Would you like a little drive into town with me" — we've only been here ten minutes.
Ray She's gotta bitta business to do and you said you wanted to buy a few things.
Brenda What's wrong with tomorrow?
Ray She's gonna take you to some nice shops, then a little look around the harbour — it'll be a nice afternoon out.   Don't be unhappy, sweetheart, don't spoil it.

She looks at him, then softens

Brenda Course I'm not unhappy. (*She kisses him*) Just promise me one thing: don't let him come The Big I Am.
Ray Bren …
Brenda And don't let him talk you into anything.
Ray Like what?
Brenda Like he always has done.

Ray It's a *holiday.*
Brenda I wonder.
Ray Sweetheart …
Brenda He owes you.   Just you remember that.

Michael comes in, grinning

Michael Not only is she giving it to him in top Spanish, she's got him
   standing to attention while she's doing it. Women. I love 'em.
Brenda We all know that, Mickey.
Michael (*grinning, pointing a finger at her, but to Ray*) Eh?   Eh?

Francine appears, taking off the hat

Francine Apparently he had the wrong invoice.
Michael How can he have the wrong invoice?
Francine Open the gates for him, will you, darling?

*Michael moves to watch the VDU and will press a button to open the
gates as:*

Francine We have to be so security-conscious.
Michael Talking of security … (*grinning*) … how about that business
   at the airport?
Brenda Yes, very funny I must say.
Michael "Would you mind coming this way, Señor?"
Ray Turned my suitcase inside out they did.
Francine I'm so sorry.
Brenda Not *your* fault, was it?
Ray I couldn't believe it — leave it out, I said, I'm on holiday.
Francine They're usually so lax.
Michael You must have a suspicious face, Raymondo. Waddaya think,
   babe — has this man got a suspicious face?
Francine Hardly.
Michael Unless of course they'd had a tip-off.
Brenda About what?
Michael I dunno.
Brenda About what?
Michael About him — say — carrying something in for someone.
Francine Not funny, Michael.
Michael I'm *serious.*
Ray Like what?
Michael Don't ask me, I'm an innocent civilian.

Ray And I'm that big a mug, am I?

Michael I'm kidding, I'm kidding.

Ray Yeah but Francine here — I mean you know …

Brenda How long have you known this man? And still you haven't learned not to jump when he rings your bell.

Ray Yeah, all right, all right. (*He grins, trying to make light of it*)

Francine Well then: if you're ready, Brenda.

Brenda Whenever you say, Francine.

Francine You're quite sure you want to come?

Brenda Oh yes — it'll give us a chance to get to know each other, won't it?

Michael I was thinking, babe: why don't you take the Merc, save me taking it down tomorrow. You can drop it off at the garridge, then when you've finished all your bits and pieces, you can give me a bell and I'll drive down and fetch you — tell you what, we'll both drive down, Ray, and I can take you all for a little drink at Pancho's.

Ray What's Pancho's then?

Michael Great little bar run by this Mexican geezer, fantastic atmosphere, best cocktails in the world, you'll love it. (*He moves away from the screen, having closed the gates*) Waddaya think, babe? (*He has taken car keys from his pocket and is holding them up*)

Francine Well it's up to Brenda and Raymond.

Brenda (*flatly*) Yeah well, it sounds a nice change from the *Dog and Duck*.

Ray Yeah — I mean — great.

Francine Well that's what we'll do then.

Francine gives Brenda a big smile and takes the car keys and:

(*Kissing his cheek*) I'll ring you. Oh and you did cancel that woman coming, did you?

Michael looks at her as though not understanding, then slaps his forehead with the butt of his hand

You've forgotten, haven't you? Oh Michael.

Michael (*to the others*) It's happening to me all the time lately — I forget things.

Francine Phone her now — where's she staying?

Michael Where was it? (*He clicks his fingers to remember*)

Francine *La Perla*.

Michael *La Perla*.

Francine It's in the book.

Michael takes up their phone book as:

He gets worse, he really does.

Michael Hang about babe, I can't change it, she's going back tomorrow.

Francine See her tomorrow then.

Michael No no I want to get it over with.

Francine Michael …

Michael I said I want to get it over with. All right? (*His look making it quite clear that there will be no more discussion on the subject*)

Francine What time is she supposed to be here?

Michael (*looking at his watch*) What time is it now — about half an hour — (*to Ray*) — I got this woman coming to see me — I forgot all about her.

Brenda Excuse me — are we in the way or something?

Michael No no no …

Francine Of course you're not in the way — and it's not that important — really — I'll tell you in the car.

Michael A little word before you go, babe … (*To Brenda and Ray*) Excuse us. (*And he turns Francine away and will speak to her quietly*) I forgot, all right babe, I forgot.

Francine Pretty, is she?

Michael Now you can stop all that — and listen — I know this is hard for you, but it's only for a coupla days, I'll give'em a few bob and pack 'em off to Laurie's hotel or something.

Francine Yes, well, we won't talk about it *here*, will we, darling? (*She holds her gracious smile whilst making it quite clear — "pas devant" — and indicates for him to come into the kitchen*)

Michael and Francine exit

When they've gone:

Ray (*quietly*) What's all *that* about?

Brenda Who knows — why don't you get out of that suit?

Ray Yeah I will in a minute — you all right for cash?

Brenda I'm fine.

Ray How much have you got?

Brenda I'm fine.

Ray Well I want you to take a bit extra…

Brenda Ray …

Ray I want you to treat yourself, buy yourself something nice — where is it, with the passports and stuff?

A slight moment and she nods and he kisses her briefly and goes upstairs

Left alone, Brenda looks around the room and takes up one of the family photographs that she is looking at when:

   Michael and Francine return

Michael Sorry about that — bitta business. Where's Ray?
Brenda Upstairs fetching something.
Francine I'll just bring the car round. (*She smiles her "lady of the house" smile at Brenda*)

   Francine goes out through the main door

Michael smiles at Brenda. She smiles back. This moment, as long as possible, and:

Michael I'm really pleased you came.
Brenda I'm really pleased you asked us.

Is she? Michael smiles and:

Michael Same old Brenda, eh? Don't give an inch.
Brenda Is that right?
Michael To *me* anyway.
Brenda Give *you* an inch, Mickey. (*This time* she *smiles*)
Michael I just want you to have a nice time.
Brenda And we will. I'm sure we will.

   Ray has been coming down the stairs

Michael (*brightly*) All right, Ray?
Ray Yeah — great.

   Francine returns

Francine Are we ready then, Brenda?
Brenda Lovely.

Ray discreetly gives Brenda folded euros. She kisses him, then briefly touches the cheek she has just kissed. A little something she's done all their lives together

Brenda And remember what I said. (*And she turns to Francine*)

Francine smiles and indicates — shall we go? And as they head out through the front door:

Francine Did you by any chance bring any flat shoes?
Brenda No, I didn't as it happens.
Francine Because I was thinking it might be an idea to buy some ...

By now they are out of sight through the front door

Michael (*calling after them*) And behave yourselves! (*He winks at Ray but his mind is on the VDU which he turns on and will remain watching to check the exit of the ladies as:*) What was all that then?
Ray What's that?
Michael "Remember what I said."
Ray (*playing for time*) Eh?
Michael Brenda.
Ray Oh — yeah. You know. Me not having a fag.
Michael Oh right. Right.

Does he believe him? This moment. Then, satisfied that the women have gone, he moves away from the VDU with:

Anyway. They'll have a nice time. Francine'll look after her.
Ray She can look after herself, Mickey: she's had a lotta practice.
Michael Yeah. You're right. She's a good girl.
Ray She's the best.

He has moved over and is looking out over the terrace

Michael Only Brenda mentioned you haven't been up to much lately. You get tired easily she says.
Ray Just been a bit run down that's all.
Michael You should come and live out here, my old mate, get some sun.
Ray I thought she didn't let you go in the sun.
Michael Lie in the sun. Lie in it.

This moment and:

Let me mark your card about me and Francine. Just so as you've got the full SP. Not only is she a very sexy lady, she is a very efficient lady. A great organizer. Well, she used to be PA to a top man so she's

the business. I like her organizing. I even let her organize *me*. That
is, I let her organize me as much as I want to be organized. So when
you say … she don't let me lie in the sun … you take my point. My
point being that if I want to lie in the sun, I lie in the fucking sun. Only
I don't want to. *I* — don't — want — to. Which is not to say I don't.
If I so choose. Right?

A slight moment

Ray Right.

*This moment — and, as though Michael's little lecture had never
happened:*

You'll want me out of the way, will you?
Michael Eh?
Ray This woman you've got coming.
Michael Oh Christ — yeah — what a berk, went clean out of me
head.
Ray Business is it?
Michael No — well — yeah, sort of — no no — as it happens, I'd like
you to be here. You might find it very entertaining.
Ray Oh yeah?
Michael I'm sitting in this little bar — Francine was away doing a
bitta business for me — and I see this pretty little thing giving me
the eyeball. I'm having me *tapas* — *boquerones*, I love *boquerones*
— and I look up and there she is coming over and I'm thinking hello
Mickey son, you're in for some nocturnal exercise … and it only turns
out she's a fucking researcher. She's over here researching this film
they're making and she starts giving me the verbals, saying how she
recognizes me and would I by any chance consider acting as Technical
Adviser. That sounds a bit iffy to me Polly I says — Polly, that's her
name, Polly — you just happen to recognize me oh no no no — and
o' course it transpires she's been sent out to find me. This film being
about the old days — and one of the characters is I quote "very loosely"
based on me and they want my OK. There'll be some money in it
of course, she says — oh well, Polly, I says, if there's some *money* in
it, like I'd do it for any other fucking reason. So she's bringing the
script over for me to have a look at and give 'em a few pointers. Pretty
little thing she is: you'll enjoy looking at her — besides which, we
can have a bit of a laugh, wind her up, give it to her large — you know
how they love it — and like you say, they don't know, the cunts, they
don't know. Anyway, she'll be here soon, we can give her the old Tom
and Geriatric double act.

Ray Sounds good — yeah — why not?
Michael Why not — right.

They sip their drinks, enjoying the thought

Ray You checked her out, did you Mickey?
Michael Checked her out?
Ray You know ...
Michael You think I'm going soft in the head or something?
Ray No — I mean — you know ...
Michael You know what?
Ray Well — young bitta skirt — it wouldn't the first time you let it
    — you know.
Michael Did I check her out? Do me a favour. (*He knocks back his
    drink*) You're not really gonna sit there sipping fucking water all day
    — have a fucking beer for chrissake.
Ray Yeah, yeah, all right, I'll have a beer.
Michael Thank Christ for that. (*He goes to the bar*)

*Ray almost takes out a cigarette but remembers and re-pockets the
packet as Michael pours two beers*

Ray takes the edge off the atmosphere with:

Ray (*lightly*) I'm not in it then. This film.
Michael Well we'll make sure you are, won't we, row you in — get you
    a few notes, pay for your holiday, yeah?
Ray Yeah, sounds good.

A moment

Michael And yeah, you're quite right, she's a little sweetheart, this
    Polly.
Ray Yeah?
Michael Bitova yaya but a very nice looker. With — reading between
    the lines and not having to put me glasses on — a penchant for the
    older man.
Ray Yeah?
Michael Putting out like a cruise liner, she was. A long 'un says I could
    have her.
Ray (*grinning*) In your dreams.
Michael In the backa my car more like and then home to mama.

*They dwell on the thought, each in his own way. And Ray says what he's
been wanting to say ever since he got here*

Ray You ever hear from Geoff? Geoff Merrison.
Michael No, not for years.   He still in the job, is he?
Ray No, no, he's retired.
Michael Now there was a copper you could do business with — what's
   he doing — security?
Ray No no — just playing golf I think.
Michael Fucking golf mad. I remember him telling me … you want to
   pull something on my patch, do it on a Wednesday afternoon — the
   whole fucking department's out on the golf course.

The door buzzer sounds. Michael looks at his watch

Michael Here we go. (*He crosses to answer the buzzer, looking at the
   VDU*) Yes?
Polly (*voice-over*) Polly Phillips to see Mr Kavanagh.

Michael winks at Ray and buzzes her in as:

Michael (*brightly*) Come on in, Polly — I'll open the gate — (*which he
   does and:*) you think they might give me some aggravation, do you?
Ray What's that?
Michael Merrison.
Ray Just wondered if you'd heard from him.
Michael Musta been for a reason.
Ray No, no, I just wondered.

*Michael opens the front door, putting on his smile, watching the unseen
Polly approach, as:*

Michael You found us all right then.
Polly (*off*) I'm a bit early, sorry.
Michael Come by taxi, did you?
Polly (*off*) I did, yes.
Michael In you come then, Polly.

   *Polly appears. She is attractive, in her late twenties, wears good cas-
   ual clothing, sandals, sunglasses, shows lots of leg and carries a small
   rucksack over one shoulder*

*Michael indicates for her to go through. She moves into the main area,
taking off her sunglasses, and sees Ray who is now standing. Michael
closes the door and moves in after her*

Ray — this is the young lady I was telling you about — Polly — er ...
Polly Phillips.
Michael Polly Phillips, Raymond Barrett.
Polly Hi.
Ray Pleased to meet you.

They shake hands rather awkwardly

Michael Raymond is one of the chaps.
Polly (*suddenly twigging*) Raymond Barrett — right.
Michael There you go Raymond, you're famous.
Ray Yeah.
Polly You were in the same gang.
Michael Firm, Polly, firm.
Ray I was his number one man.
Michael I was the brains, Raymond was the brawn.
Ray ("*smiling*") Yeah.
Michael Sit yourself down.
Polly Thank you. (*She sits, putting the rucksack close beside her*)

Michael winks at Ray

Polly, although bright, seems very ingenuous. Slightly threatened but fascinated in equal measure. Michael and Ray are well-aware of this — used to it, in fact — and enjoy themselves by acting up their parts, exaggerating as and when it amuses or suits them to do so

Michael Ray's first time out here, innit Ray?
Ray It is, yeah.
Michael I thought it might be good if he sat in, Polly.
Polly Um — yes — yes — great.
Michael Unless you ...
Polly No — absolutely.
Michael There y'go, Raymondo — sorted.
Ray You're sure, Polly?
Michael Course she's sure — and in case you're wondering, Polly, the girls have had to go into town.
Polly Yes I think we passed them — a Mercedes?
Michael The Merc, yeah — Francine — my wife — sends her apologies and says she looks forward to meeting you later.
Polly That's nice.

Michael Just as long as you don't mind being stuck on your own with a couple of old has-beens.
Polly No I mean it's — you know — I mean — absolutely.
Michael So then: what can I get you to drink?
Polly Umm — glass of white wine?
Michael I've got a very nice little Rioja Blanco Barrica — how would that suit you?
Polly Sounds great.
Michael Gonna have a beer with us, are you, Raymond?
Ray Uh — yeah — why not?
Michael Why not he says.

Michael goes through into the kitchen

Ray sits. They exchange uncomfortable little smiles

Michael (*off*) How much did he charge you?
Polly Sorry?
Michael (*off*) The taxi.
Polly Oh umm — eight euros.
Michael (*off*) You come from the hotel, did you?
Polly Yuh.
Michael (*off*) Yeah, eight's about right.

Again Polly and Ray exchange an awkward little smile

Ray Mickey says you're doing a film.
Polly For Channel Four, yes.
Ray What company are you with then?
Polly Wishbone.
Ray Don't think I know them.
Michael (*off*) Ray's done some film work, haven't you Ray?
Ray I have as it happens, yeah. Wishbone.
Polly Wishbone, yes.

Michael comes in carrying a small tray on which are an open bottle of white wine, a wine glass, a bowl of nuts, a bowl of olives, some napkins, some bottles of beer, an opener

Michael He was an extra in that wassisname's film, wassisname — married to wassername.
Polly Oh right — right.
Ray And a coupla other things. Mostly telly.

Polly Acting, you mean.

Ray No, no, in an advisory capacity.

Polly It's very good of you to see me like this.

Michael (*pouring wine for her*) I could never say no to a beautiful young lady.

Polly I really appreciate it.

He gives her the wine, toasts her with his beer. Ray toasts her with his empty glass. They drink

Polly Mm, lovely.

Michael Have an olive, they're from my own farm.

Polly I will do. Thank you. (*She smiles*)

He smiles back

Michael So then, Polly. Where's this script you want me to look at?

Glad of a change of atmosphere, she quickly pulls a document from her rucksack as:

Polly Well I have to like be honest and say that it isn't like really so much a script as a sort of like a storyline.

Michael Are you saying you told me a little porkie, Polly?

Polly Well yes — well no — there *was* a script but everyone hated it so they like got someone in to do some twiddling but he like hated it so much he said he'd only do it if he could like start again from the top so um … anyway. This is like the new storyline. Well, as it stands at the moment.

She gives it to him, somewhat apprehensively. He takes it and holds it as though it's a newborn child

Michael Look at this, Raymond. This is where it all begins. (*He shakes his head admiringly at the script and:*) You want me to have a look at it now, do you?

Polly Well — no — whenever.

Michael Right. (*He sets the document, over-respectfully, down on a side table as:*)

Polly It's like very rough — just a sort of scene by scene breakdown — and even then very much — you know — nothing set in concrete.

Michael Nevertheless … I look forward to reading it.

Polly What we were hoping is that you could like um you know, make a few suggestions.

Michael Absolutely Polly.

Polly For a fee of course.

Michael For a fee — of course.

Polly Anything you disagree with — you know ——

Michael Absolutely.

Polly You will of course have script approval. I mean like — you know — anything to do with your character. Or anything else, really.

Michael (*very "seriously"*) Oh yes, I'd have to have script approval. I always have script approval — you do an' all, don't you, Ray? (*He gives him a wink*)

Ray I always have it put in the contract, yeah, definitely.

Michael Tell you a little story, Polly ... first time I was involved doing a film, this producer geezer says to me you can of course have script approval and being new at the game I says what does that mean? And he says it means if there's something you don't like you can have it changed and I says if there's something I don't like I'll tear your arms off.

Polly has listened to this, rapt

Michael Only joshing o' course, but it done the business, didn't it Ray?

Ray Oh yes, it done the business.

Michael Seriously though, Polly... we know you have to indulge in what you call artistic licence and we understand it.

Ray We do yes.

Michael But what we will not tolerate ... is the taking of liberties.

Ray No way.

Michael For example, I don't do documentaries no more.

Ray Never.

Michael Because people twist things, you see Polly.

Ray Edit things so that you look like you're saying what you're not saying.

Michael They can have this interviewer saying — without you even being there — "did you enjoy torturing so-and-so?" — someone you've never met, let alone plugged into the electrics — and then they put in this shot of you grinning all over your face at something humorous that was said earlier and you come out looking like some sort of animal, some sort of callous animal.

Ray They set you up, Polly, and then they stab you in the back.

Michael The point being this, Polly: we never asked for the glamour.

Ray Never.

Michael It was the media who glamorized crime, Polly.

Ray Fleas, Polly. Leeches. No disrespect.

Michael However ... however ... the one thing you people do get right is the loyalty. The respect. Raymond knows what I'm saying, don't you Ray?

Ray You see, Polly ... you had hard men, soft men, educated men, men who couldn't spell their own name. But we all had one thing in common.

Michael Loyalty, Polly. Trust.

Ray You knew who you could depend on. You knew who would never let you down. Come what.

Michael Come what.

Ray We had a code, you see Polly.

Michael Absolutely.

Ray Respect ... reputation ... tradition.

This moment and:

Polly And you think that's ... you think that's changed ...

Michael (*scornfully*) Has it changed, Raymond?

Ray Drugs ... kidnapping .... abusing little kids ... turning over old ladies ... these people aren't villains, Polly, not proper villains, they're scum, opportunistic scum.

Michael I mean, let's face it, you bend a football and your wife and kids have to have a bodyguard.

Ray It's all about drugs, drugs have changed everything.

Michael I was reading about this microchip thing someone's invented to monitor the whereabouts of little children. What sort of world is that? Mind you, I'd put money into it — I mean, be fair. (*He smiles*)

This moment. It's like they're waiting for her to make the next move. And, finally:

Polly Well then I'll umm ... I'll like wait to hear from you, shall I?

Michael Is that it then, Polly? You don't want to ask us no more questions?

Polly Well I mean if you — don't mind.

Michael Course we don't mind, do we Raymond?

Ray Course not.

Michael Just as long as Raymond can ask *you* a few questions first.

Polly Sorry?

Michael The thing is — despite all my assurances — Raymond isn't sure that you are who you say you are.

Polly Sorry?

Ray It's all right Mickey — I'm happy.

Michael No no, be fair Raymond ... you see, Polly ... Raymond is a little concerned that I have let my shall-we-say natural inclinations run away with me and that you might be — well, let's be honest — up to no good.

Ray (*awkwardly*) You see, Polly ... people like us ... you can never be too careful ...

Polly You mean ... you think I might show you in a bad light. I mean no, I mean that's why ——

Michael What he means Polly is that you might have nothing to do with making a film at all.

Polly But I've shown you the script.

Michael Anyone can show us a script, Polly, scripts are ten a penny nowadays.

Polly And you like ... phoned the office and everything.

Michael That's what I told him — but Raymond is a very suspicious person. D'you know, there was a bloke come here earlier to deliver some flowers and Raymond is convinced he's up to something naughty.

Ray (*trying to make light*) Leave it out, Mickey.

Michael Wass he gonna do, I said ... batter me to death with a geranium? (*He grins, pleased with his joke — and not a little pleased at making Ray look something of a berk*)

Ray Listen. It's all right. I'm happy.

Michael You're sure — I mean I don't want your stomach getting all upset again.

Ray I'm happy.

Michael Just as long as when she pulls out a gun and blows your head off it's not down to *me*, all right? However, Polly, however ... Raymond is quite right ... you cannot be too careful — which is why I never skimp when it comes to insurance.

During this, he has taken up the remote control. The screen comes on and he jump cuts it through to a playback of their earlier exchange

Ray (*on screen*) Mickey says you're doing a film.

Polly (*on screen*) For Channel Four, yes.

Michael operates the remote so that Polly's "For Channel Four — yes" is repeated twice. Then turns off the picture and:

Michael All there for prosperity. So if you aren't who you say you are, Polly, now might be a good time to drink up and catch the next plane home otherwise ... otherwise ... you might be getting yourself a little visit. (*He smiles*)

Ray has been as surprised as Polly by this little performance

Not that it will come to that, of course it won't. But now we all know where we stand. (*Again the "smile" and:*) So then Polly ... what else can we tell you?

She gulps down some wine and is now reaching into her rucksack

Polly Is it all right if I use a tape recorder? (*She produces one*)
Michael Don't see why not — Ray?
Ray No problem.
Polly What I'd like to do first is like get some sort of — background stuff — you know — sort of like general stuff.
Michael Absolutely .
Polly So as I um see it ... you sort of like drifted into crime ...
Michael And we sort of like didn't drift out again — correct.
Ray Mind you, things were different in them days.
Michael Not many.
Ray Not that we're making excuses.
Michael In our book, excuses is a form of masturbation if you'll pardon my Spanish.
Ray What is done is done, Polly.
Michael But they were, things were different.
Ray I mean, you take Old Bill. How many coppers you meet today have ever felt a collar?
Michael See Polly ... in our day, the psychology of the criminal and the copper were very similar.
Ray Either of 'em could have gone either way.
Michael A good copper would have made a good villain and *vice versa*.
Ray What you might call a career choice.
Michael Nowadays they come straight out of university clutching their degree in Sociology and fast-track it straight to Head of CID.
Ray How can you deal with a man like that, a man with no real feel for the game?
Polly Are you saying umm ...
Michael We had coppers on the payroll. Yes, Polly. That side of the business never changes. You could buy a copper then, you can buy a copper now. Or so we understand, don't we Raymond?
Ray Oh yes. So we understand.

They smile at Polly, raising eyebrows. This moment and:

Michael Oh and a small but important point. We were villains, Polly.
We were not gangsters. (*He reaches across, takes her tape recorder
and speaks directly into it*) Do not ever call us gangsters. (*He returns
the recorder to her*)
Polly So um ...you sort of like drifted into crime and then did sort of
like mainly robberies and things.
Michael Crimes for which we were punished, Polly.
Ray We done our crime, we done our time.
Michael But yes, we were robbers ... banks ... security vans ... gold
bullion.
Ray But never from the ordinary man.
Michael The ordinary man gets robbed by the Chancellor of the
Exchequer, not by the likes of us.
Polly Great! (*She notes it down as:*)
Michael However, we were not angels, Polly. On occasions, it was
necessary to give a man a slap.   But never without good reason.
Ray It's like Jack used to say. Jack Spot. Hit 'em hard.
Michael Hit 'em hard and they won't come back for more.
Ray So in a way, you might say we was minimizing the physical side
of things.
Michael Mind you, there were some nutcases.
Ray Look at Frankie, Frankie was outrageous.
Michael But in the main, yeah, all right, there was a touch of violence.
Ray But only amongst your own, and only as a last resort.
Michael Precisely.
Ray What you needed to build up, you see Polly, was a reputation.
Michael Listen to this, Polly: Raymond in his time was a very hard
man.
Ray I was.
Michael He was so hard he used Jeyes Fluid as an aftershave.
Ray (*grinning*) Still do as it happens.
Michael Oh yes, Raymond here was well hard.
Ray You see Polly ... it's not so much actual violence as the threat of
violence. The knowledge of what a man is capable of.
Michael Let me tell you, Polly: when I first come here, my reputation
preceded me if you understand — and yes, all right, I played up to
it. Which made it a lot easier to negotiate certain little — business
arrangements. But actual violence — your physical violence — never.
Someone fronts me, I don't get involved, I walk away. It's all behind
me. It's another world.

The telephone rings

Can't be the girls already ... Excuse me. (*He moves to answer the phone. Into it*) Yes? ... Ah — *si* — (*cupping the phone; to Ray and Polly*) — garridge, about the car ... (*back into the phone*) *Si. ... Que tipo de problema?* ... *Si.* ... *Si.* ... (*Cupping the phone as he listens*) Tell Polly about that lunatic Billy — little story you might use, Polly.

And he continues "Si ... Si"ing into the phone, slowly walking out on to the terrace and out of sight

An awkward little moment and:

Ray He's a right card.
Polly Yes.
Ray Always has been.

She nods, smiles

Fantastic sense of humour.
Polly Yes.
Ray He loves winding people up. You know. Having a bit of a laugh.

An awkward little moment

But underneath it all he's the main man. The real business. I'd do anything for him.

Another awkward little moment

Polly What's this story? About Billy. Sorry.
Ray Well it's an example of how like not to be. How things can — you know — get out of hand.

She waits. And:

That thing off, is it?

She holds up the tape recorder, indicating that it is off. A moment and:

Ray We're sitting there, you see, in Billy's flat — there's Billy, me and this bit of a loudmouth called Keith and Keith starts going on about his brother and all the money he's making. The thing being that up until then he'd never even mentioned a brother. Never even mentioned one. No. So. We're sitting there and he says, this Keith, my brother Paul wrote to me yesterday, he's getting married in Coventry Cathedral and

Billy says what brother Paul? and he says my brother Paul, I just said didn't I and Billy says you haven't got a brother and he says what do you mean I haven't got a brother and Billy says what do you mean what do I mean and Billy says I'm saying, you've never mentioned having a brother in fact in fact you've never mentioned having a brother or a sister or anyone and he says you've never mentioned that two hundred quid you owe me but it don't mean to say you don't owe it to me and I say hold on hold on sensing something nasty about to occur but Billy says what two hundred quid and he says bleep off that two hundred quid you owe me and Billy says are you talking about the seven bleeping dwarves and he says that's right the seven bleeping dwarves only you could only get six of them, couldn't you, you couldn't get bleeping Bashful and I said come on chaps that wasn't a real bet that was a jest and he says it wouldn't have been a bleeping jest if the so-and-so had won, you bleeping ... and then he calls Billy the c word and Billy tells him, I hate the c word, I do, I bleeping hate it so I says to him take that back and he says like bleep I will and he says it again so Billy chins him. Now you would have thought you would have thought that would be it, wouldn't you? You would have thought he would have got up said fair dos and had a drink or something but what does he do? He goes out and he comes back with a bleeping hammer doesn't he? I'm in the toilet at the time — I've always suffered from a bitta stomach trouble — but I can hear it all going on ... I'm gonna bleeping kill you he says, you get right up my bleeping nose you do ... and out comes the c word again so Billy sees red doesn't he? And before you know it he's got the hammer off him and he's caving his bleeping head in and he's lying there bubbling burgundy. So I come out of the toilet and I says now look what you've gone and done I said and I've got to be honest, I almost used the c word myself. Keith just lies there staring up at us, all this red bubbling out of his mouth then he gives a great big — he passes wind and that's it, he's with his maker. Well. You can imagine. I'm horrified. Well there's blood everywhere and half-past ten Billy's wife's coming back from Tenerife with the kids, I mean we're gonna have our time cut out getting rid of the body let alone bleeping re-decorating so nothing for it but on the blower to Danny, Danny Marterolli — and ten minutes later he's round with two of the lads and they're scrubbing their — whatsits off. Good as gold, Danny — and a right card. Bucket and mop and singing away he is ...I'm gonna wash that man right out of this flat, I'm gonna wash that man right out of this flat and send him on his way. He had a really nice voice, Danny, really nice, I think he would have gone a long way if that had been his career route, mind you his mother used to play the piano for Charlie Chester so it was in the family you might say.

Where was I? Oh yeah, Keith. Three hours later he's all bundled up and in the back of the motor and we're taking him to well that I cannot divulge if you don't mind, Polly. Anyway, Cynthia comes back, his wife, and all she says is oh what a lovely smell, we did, we did it out spotless. Course, the cozzers give Billy a pull but he's at the airport all day waiting for his wife, isn't he, with me and Danny as witnesses. They've never found Keith and they never will but here's the funny part, here's the really funny part ... I found out he did have a brother. Keith. Only his name was Leslie. Not Paul. Leslie. Now why was that? Why would he not mention his brother and then when he does mention him, call him another name? Anyway. That's what I mean. That is an example of how these things happen. And how you do not call someone the c word, not under any circumstances.

Michael comes back in

Michael Everywhere you go it's the same, innit? You take it in for a fifty-p windscreen wiper and you end up lobbing out a fistfulla notes for a setta new tyres. Did you tell her?
Ray About Billy? — Yeah.
Michael Any good? I mean, something you can work into the script?
Polly I mean — yes — great.
Michael It's these little touches that give it authenticity, innit?
Polly Absolutely.
Michael That's what you want, isn't it Polly — authenticity.
Polly Oh — yes — absolutely.
Michael Or what passes for it. Eh Polly? (*He "smiles"*) So then. What else can we tell you?
Polly Umm ... oh yes, while I remember it (*flicking through her notebook*) ... one of your associates was a man called ... ummm ... (*finding the name*) ... Manzi, Anthony Manzi ...

This moment

Michael Yeah, Tony Manzi. Not an associate, Polly, but yeah I knew him.
Polly I understand — sorry — I understand that you did business with him.

Michael and Ray exchange a brief look

Michael That is a popular misconception, Polly.
Polly But you know he disappeared.

Michael Course I know he disappeared.

Ray What's this all about? (*He is clearly more anxious to know than Michael*)

Polly Can I ask you not to say anything?

Michael Scouts' honour.

Polly (*excited at passing such information*) Well I was like talking to a policeman — detective — you know — my research — and he said — they've like found his body — Anthony Manzi — and they like think he was murdered.

Michael A policeman told you.

Polly Yes.

Michael That was very indiscreet of him.

Polly I think he was trying to impress me.

Ray What's this got to do with *us* Polly?

Polly I was like wondering whether it was like something we could use in the film.

Michael That would be up to you, wouldn't it? (*He gives her his smile*) Anything else we can help you with, is there Polly?

Polly Well umm — you know — the time you spent in prison — your family and everything — if um you know if you like had any regrets.

Michael Our life of crime you mean.

Polly Well — yes.

Michael Ray?

A moment. And Ray gives a little shake of the head. Whether it means he has no regrets or that he doesn't want to say, we don't know

Michael Regrets? Yeah, one or two, who hasn't? Would I have chosen another way of life? All things considered, Polly, and hand on my heart, I have to say no.

Polly So why did you stop?

The sheer — and typical — naïvety causes pause

Michael Why did I stop?

Polly Yes. Sorry.

Michael Why did I retire?

Polly Yes.

Michael I "retired", Polly, because I was moving more and more into legitimate business. A kinda natural progression you might say.

Polly But nevertheless based on the proceeds of crime. The legitimate business. Sorry.

Michael (*holding his hands up*) Why would I deny it? All I've got, all you see, is the result of villainy. I'm sending my grandson to a private school on the proceeds of villainy — just like these robber barons who got their start doing a bitta business for the royal incumbent so where's the difference and am I ashamed? Am I ... (*were he not in the presence of a lady, is he bollocks*). Listen. Polly. Why are you here? Because you're gonna make a picture. What's it about, this picture? It's about crime, it's about villainy. And what do you want this picture to have — apart from the artistic integrity you people are always banging on about — a large profit margin, that's what you want it to have. In other words, you're making money out of crime. Like I say — you — all the media — I mean look at television — and — if we want to look a bit further — coppers, councillors, members of Parliament, all taking backhanders ... all those gents who shlep up to the city so they can have a nice day manipulating the market, another million for them another overdraft for the mug with his two point eight kids and no future ... we could go on forever about proceeds of crime, couldn't we Polly my love?

Polly I suppose if you ...

Michael I've got two brothers, one of them's an accountant the other one's a solicitor. Which of the three of us has made the most money outa crime, would you reckon? Eh? Eh?

This moment ... A mobile phone rings

Polly I think that's mine — sorry — (*she takes it out, looks at the display*) Oh God, it's my mother — I'm so sorry — d'you mind if I ...

Michael Not at all.

Polly gets up, speaking into the phone as she moves on to the terrace and out of sight, with:

Polly Hi Ma. No I'm cool, cool ...

Polly goes

Ray Christ, Mickey.

Michael What?

Ray *Manzi*.

Michael So they've found his body.

Ray Because — and between you and me — right — I haven't said nothing to Bren — I thought that might be why you asked me out here.

Michael What the fuck are you talking about?

Ray Merrison told me — about them finding the body — I thought he
might have marked your card.
Michael I told you — I haven't spoken to him.
Ray Yeah but ...
Michael It's fucking history — years ago — forget about it.
Ray   Yeah. Well.
Michael "Yeah — well — yeah well" ... I tell you this, Ray — you
might have got older but you ain't got less twitchy — no wonder you
need a fucking prescription.

Polly comes in

Polly Sorry about that.
Michael Mothers eh, Polly?
Ray Listen, I — er — (*standing*) — I think I'll get out of this suit. Er
— nice meeting you, Polly — er — excuse me. (*And he moves away
but:*)
Michael You all right, Ray?
Ray Yeah, 'course I'm all right.   Just need to get out of this suit.

Ray goes up the stairs and out of sight

Michael Wouldn't surprise me if he has a little sleep.
Polly Right.
Michael He gets tired.
Polly Right.
Michael And he's not been too well I understand. (*He takes up the
remote control and activates the television*)

*First we see the the split-screen image, then a full screen image of a
bedroom.   Ray comes into the room.   He sits on the edge of the bed,
wearily*

That man was as strong as an ox. I've seen him ... (*He mimes two
bunched fists. But:*)   Getting old.   Not much to recommend it, I
promise you. (*He smiles*)

The telephone rings

Telephones. Where would we be without'em?   Excuse me. (*He
answers the telephone*) Yes? ... Oh hallo babe, listen, there's been a
change a plan, Raymond's having a little lie down. ... No, no, just a bit
tired, tell her, so what I'll do is come down on my own. ... Yeah, she

is. ...   No, not really. ... Well if it's all right with *you*. ... Yeah — I'll
leave now. ... Yeah. ... Love you. (*He replaces the receiver*) I'm
gonna have to drive into town.
Polly Oh — right.
Michael I'll only be half an hour or so, why don't you help yourself
to a drink, have a chat with Raymond if and when he comes down,
otherwise you can sit here and watch the telly or something.
Polly Are you sure?
Michael Sure I'm sure. Then you can have a little bite with us —
we're gonna have a barbecue and watch the fireworks — there's a big
firework display down on the beach.
Polly Will that be all right with your wife?
Michael Her idea.

After a moment, Polly nods and:

Polly Great.
Michael She's a very bright lady, my wife. Doesn't miss much. I have
to be very careful. If anyone buzzes the gate, ignore it. (*He makes to
go but stops, comes back, and leans over the back of her chair with:*)
Something you and your associates should bear in mind, Polly. I am,
if crossed, not a nice man. I am not — nice.

This moment

And he goes out through the main door

*She remains where she is for a moment, then she takes up the remote
control and activates the screen, moving to stand in front of it.   The
split screen images appear and she changes it to a single shot of Michael
walking to his (second) car and then to a single shot of the bedroom ...
which is now empty*

*During this, we, but not she, will have seen Ray coming slowly down
the stairs. He is now wearing a long-sleeved shirt and casual trousers. Very chain store. He stands for a moment, looking at her. She
becomes aware and turns off the television as:*

Polly You caught me playing with his toys.
Ray I did, didn't I?
Polly He's gone to pick up his wife.
Ray Oh yeah?
Polly They've invited me to stay and have a meal.

Ray Nice.

She sits.   He sits.   There is an awkward silence.   He sits turning the packet of cigarettes in his hand

Polly Can I ask you something?
Ray What's that?
Polly Why you think I would — well lie — about who I am?
Ray Just — something I heard, that's all.
Polly About me?
Ray No no. Just something I heard. I was out of order, forget it. (*He smiles, but again finds himself turning the cigarette packet*)
Polly But — sorry — you think I could have been an unwelcome visitor.

He considers and:

Ray The thing is … you lead the sort of life we've led … you can't help but make enemies. On both sides of the law. So, retired or not, you're always looking over your shoulder.
Polly Is that why he's so security-conscious?
Ray Maybe.

This moment.   And then she attempts to make light of it with:

Polly Mind you … all the security they've got … I think even the SAS would have trouble breaking in.
Ray Yeah.

They smile. And then he is standing and:

Ray I think I'll just go for a little walk round the garden.
Polly Oh — right.
Ray I could do with a bit of air.
Polly Right.
Ray I mean if that …
Polly No no, I've got a couple of calls to make. (*She indicates her mobile*)

This moment. Then he nods and almost goes out on to the terrace but:

Ray There's always a way in, Polly. It's doing what you came to do and getting out.

This moment and then he goes, taking out a cigarette

Polly sits for a moment.   Then she moves to the terrace to watch his departure. Satisfied, she takes out a mobile telephone and keys in a pre-set number as she returns to sit. A moment and:

Polly (*into the phone*) It's me. ... Yeah, no problem.   So far, just sitting here looking suitably impressed while they go through their Morecombe and Wise routine. ... Yeah, very funny. Be a lot funnier if Eric knew that Ernie was selling him down the river. (*She listens, smiling at something that is said to her, and:*)

CURTAIN

ACT II

The same. Later that evening

Dark outside, illuminated here and there by garden lights. There are a dining table and chairs on the terrace. The table bears the remains of an informal barbecue meal, some low-burning candles. Polly's rucksack is propped up against a chair

Ray sits in the sitting-room, staring into his glass of water

Michael appears on the terrace. He wears an apron, has barbecue tongs in one hand, a glass of whisky in the other. He stands looking at Ray — who is unaware of him — and then comes in

Michael Where's Brenda?
Ray Upstairs getting my pills.

Michael nods and:

Michael You've hardly said a word all night, something on your mind, is there?
Ray No no, just a bit — you know — a bit tired.
Michael You know what *I* think, Raymond? I think you're still fretting about this Manzi business.
Ray I just think we should talk about it, Mickey.
Michael It's fucking history. Forget it. (*He glances outside*) Francine's no mug — she can tell when something's going on and I don't want her upset so wake your fucking ideas up. (*And he turns on his smile as:*)

Francine and Polly come in from the terrace, each holding a glass

Michael Waddaya think of the pool then, Polly?
Polly Fantastic.
Michael Gonna have a little swim are you?
Francine Later maybe — where's Brenda?

Ray makes to tell her but:

Michael Getting Raymond's medication — tell you what, babe, I've got two lovely little bitsa steak left — seems a pity to waste 'em.

Francine They won't *be* wasted, darling — we can have them tomorrow in a sandwich or something.

Michael You're right, babe, you are absolutely right. (*He points the tongs at her*) This woman, doctor's daughter, always had enough food on the table, never had to skimp on anything. D'you know what she does?

Francine I don't think they'll be all that interested, do you, darling?

Michael Course they'll be interested — d'you know what she does? She turns the tomato sauce bottle upside down to get the last drop out of it. *All* the bottles. Mayonnaise, sauce, shampoo ... because that's the way she was brought up, that's what her mother used to do. My mother, bless her, day to day, hand to mouth, something like that would never occur to her. Never occur to her. In fact, if it did occur to her, she wouldn't do it because it would let the neighbours know how skint we were. Right, Raymond?

Ray Right, Mickey.

Michael In fact Polly, my family was so skint, Christmas time I used to get an erection just so I'd have something to play with. Boom-boom.

Francine Yes darling, now go and boom-boom your barbecue.

Michael toasts her with his whisky and grins. Francine gives an exaggerated but not heavy eyes-to-heaven look at Polly

During this, Brenda has come down the stairs. She comes in, carrying a bottle of pills

Michael Here she is ... who needs BUPA when you've got Brenda, eh Raymond?

Brenda ignores this, gives the pills to Ray. He gives her a little smile of thanks

Brenda Did you take one dinnertime?

Ray I did, yeah.

Michael What are they for this time?

Brenda How d'you mean — this time?

Michael Be fair, Brenda — he's *always* taking pills.

Brenda How would you know, you haven't seen him for two years.

Francine Go and do your barbecue.

For a moment it looks as though Michael will reply in kind to Brenda, but instead, smiles and goes out on to the terrace and out of sight

Ray He's a card, innee?
Francine Oh yes — never a dull moment.
Brenda Have you been smoking?
Ray No.
Brenda Well someone has — take your pill.

She refills his glass of water as he tips a pill from the bottle as:

Polly How did you meet? You and Michael.
Francine Mmm? Oh ... we were introduced by a mutual friend. I was
on my own, Michael was on his own, so ... you know ...
Michael (*off, calling*) Raymond?
Ray (*calling back*) What's that, Mickey?
Michael (*off*) Come here a second, will you?
Ray Right. (*He quickly drinks down the pill and gives the bottle to
Brenda*)

Ray goes onto the terrace and out of sight

*Brenda, still holding the pills, will move across to look out over the ter-
race as:*

Francine So we ... went out to dinner and so on and ... well ... he's a
very attractive man.   As I'm sure you agree.
Polly Umm — well — yes.
Francine Yes. And he *is* inclined to — wag his tail — at the slightest
flattery.   Especially from silly young women.   I have to make very
sure I keep my eye on him. (*She "smiles".   But the warning is clear*)
Polly When you say "on your own" ...
Francine Is this part of your research? (*She smiles, but with an edge*)
Polly No, I just ...
Francine I mean there was no-one else in my life.   Isn't that what one
usually means when one says ...
Polly I'm sorry, I meant ...
Francine You meant what was someone like me doing out here on her
own.
Polly Well — yes — I suppose I ...
Francine Starting again.   How's that?

*Michael and Ray come into view on the terrace. Michael is no longer
wearing the apron but is holding his glass. Michael is speaking quietly
to Ray who seems reticent about something*

Brenda What are you two arguing about?
Michael Arguing, who's arguing, we're working out a plan to kidnap
Prince Edward — right, Raymond?

Ray Right.

Michael Our idea being ... not to ask for a ransom but to see how long it is before anyone notices.

Francine He's a very nice young man.

Brenda Yeah. If you like a drink on a stick.

Michael gives Ray a wink, and will replenish his whisky as:

Michael I was thinking ... d'you remember that party I had just before I come out here?

Ray I do — that was a really good party, wasn't it, Bren?

Brenda (*flat*) Fantastic.

Michael One of my best.

Ray I think you're right.

Michael I done a barbecue then.

Ray You did.

Michael That was when I lived in Wimbledon, Polly.

Francine Excuse me.

She goes into the kitchen as:

Ray Beautiful house that was, beautiful. How many bedrooms was it, Mickey?

Brenda Eight.

Michael (*grinning*) See? She remembers.

Brenda Well you told me often enough.

Ray Eight bedrooms — fantastic.

Michael We had some great parties in that house.

Ray Mickey was renowned for his parties, Polly.

Michael I was.

Francine appears, pulling on a pair of Marigold gloves. She moves towards the terrace

Where you going, babe?

Francine To clear the dishes.

Michael No no babe, I'll do it later.

Francine I'll do it now, thank you.

Polly Can I help you?

Francine No thank you, Polly, I'm fine. (*Quietly, to Michael*) Don't drink too much, darling, you get silly.

She goes on to the terrace, puts out the candles and starts clearing the table

Ray Sorry, Mick.

Michael What's that?

Ray Talking about — you know — in front of Francine.

Michael Yeah — you're right — (*calling*) sorry babe.

Francine What for this time?

Michael Talking about — you know.

Francine (*coming in with plates*) The thing about going down Memory
   Lane is that you never know quite where it might lead.   Darling — I
   really don't mind you talking about "the old days" as long as you do
   it with a certain amount of discretion and don't expect me to join in.
   But then how could I?

Brenda Anyway … I would have thought this was all very useful to
   you, Polly. Background stuff. Character stuff. Michael and his parties,
   Raymond and his pills. The criminal as human being. (*She "smiles"
   at Francine*) Are you sure you don't want a hand?

Francine No no I'm fine. (*She gives Brenda her gracious smile*) Thank
   you.

*During the following she will move between terrace and kitchen with
dishes and so on*

Ray Yeah, they were fantastic, those parties.

Michael We used to get all sorts.

Ray You did.

Michael A nice mix.

Ray They were.

Michael A lotta showbiz people used to come.

Ray They did — yeah.

Michael Lionel Bart.

Ray Lionel. God bless him.

Michael Alma.

Ray Alma. God bless her. What was it they called her again?

Brenda The girl with the giggle in her voice.

Ray That's it. The girl with the giggle in her voice.

Michael (*to Polly*) She was a singer.

Ray She had this giggle in her voice.

Michael Died very young. Well, Lionel was no age, was he?

Ray No, no he wasn't.

Michael Stanley.

Ray Stanley?

Michael Stanley Baker. Now he *was* a hard man. He could have been
   one of us.

Ray You're right, he could.

Michael He died an' all.

Brenda Are you sure you don't want a hand, Francine?

Francine No really I'm fine.

Ray Little Jimmy Jinx.

Michael Little Jimmy Jinx. Yeah.

Ray He was a boxer.

Michael Never won a fight.

Brenda He got knocked down so often he had a cauliflower bum.

Ray Who else used to come?

Michael That wassisname, the big bloke, the MP.

Ray Oh — yeah — wassisname.

Michael What *was* his name…?

Ray Beatty … Booty …

Brenda Boothby.

Michael That's it, Boothby, wassisname Boothby.

Brenda Robert.

Michael That's him, Robert.

Ray Loved the twins, you know, Polly.

Brenda How could you not?

Ray Loved 'em.

Michael Supposed to have been wassisname's illegitimate son, you know.

Ray Who?

Michael Boothby.

Ray No — whose son?

Brenda Churchill, Winston Churchill.

Ray No.

Michael So they say.

Ray Winston Churchill?

Michael Winston Churchill.

Ray I didn't know that.

Unseen by the others, Michael gives a slight raise of the hand to Ray and briefly mimes using a telephone — a signal we'll come to understand later — and:

Michael Yes, Polly … we had guests from all different walks of life but they all had one thing in common, they all liked a good knees-up.

Ray And you used to give 'em a good knees-up an' all.

Michael No expense spared.

Brenda Yes, Mickey, I'll give you that, you always knew how to put your hand in your pocket.

Michael (*making it sound light*) Give me that, give me that? Meaning what, Bren?

Ray Meaning you was always very generous.
Michael Oh — right — *right*. (*He gives a little jerk of the head at Ray*)

The others do not see this movement

Ray will move away as:

Ray Tell you who I often think about — Benny Verner — you remember little Benny, Bren.
Brenda (*flat*) The life and soul.
Ray That's what brought him to mind ... (*To Polly*) He used to play the spoons.
Brenda Him and his ... spoons.
Ray You know ... (*He mimes for Polly playing the spoons and:*) "Blaze Away", "My Yiddishe Mama", he could do the lot ...
Brenda Not only could — did.
Ray Any sorta gathering, out would come his spoons. Used to go down a treat.
Brenda It didn't go down a treat the day they buried his mother.
Ray No, that was a bit out of order, I must say.

The gate buzzer sounds. Michael and Francine exchange a look — who's this? Michael, who is standing near the buzzer, answers it, checking the VDU

Michael Hallo?

No answer

Hola — quien es? (*And he decides that:*) It'll be those kids mucking about. (*And he explains*) Local kids playing silly buggers. We get a lot of it lately. (*To Francine*) What do I do with 'em?

She takes the telephone from him and:

Francine (*into the phone*) Iros o llamo a la policia. (*She hangs up*)
Michael Don't matter about the police, they'll have *me* to deal with — now then — we all right for drinks, are we?
Brenda Yes.

They indicate that they are. Michael replenishes his own glass

Polly How long have you been here?

Michael The house — or Spain?

Polly Both.

Michael How long have we had this house, babe?

Francine Two years in March.

Michael Spain … what — five, six years.

Polly And was there like you know any particular reason you came here — to Spain.

Michael Where *all* the naughty boys come, innit?

Polly No I mean …

Michael (*grinning*) What you mean is, Polly, was I having it on my heels from the Old Bill. No Polly, I was not.

Brenda It was because of his wife.

Ray (*quietly*) Leave it out, Bren.

Brenda Well wasn't it?

Ray Yeah but … (*He indicates Francine*)

Brenda That's right, isn't it, Mickey, you came here because of Cheryl.

Michael looks at Brenda

Michael That's exactly right, Brenda. Exactly right.

Brenda (*to Polly*) She wasn't well. His wife.

Michael No. She wasn't well. Listen, if you don't mind, I'd rather …

Francine I don't mind, darling — really. (*She kisses him lightly*) Go on — tell her — or perhaps *you'd* rather do it, Brenda?

She makes it sound light but they all get the point

Michael Cheryl — my first wife — had a very weak chest. Funny that — lovely strong girl, never smoked in her life, but she had this very weak chest. Every winter she'd get these terrible bouts of bronchitis and every year they got worse so in the end the specialist says listen, the best thing you can do is try somewhere warmer. Well, we'd been out here before visiting some of the chaps and we liked it so we thought, give it a try, why not, we can always go back if we don't like it, so … you know. Anyway. We'd been here about what nine months and she was out doing a bitta shopping and this lorry went outa control and … bang, she was dead. I took her home and buried her next to her mum and dad. Well, she wouldn't have wanted to be buried here.

Brenda No. She wouldn't.

Michael No. And tell the truth, once she'd gone bless her, there didn't seem much point coming back here.

Brenda But you did come back.

He looks at her

Michael Yeah. I came back. I had things to settle. And it was the
luckiest thing I did because I met Francine. (*He lightly kisses her
brow*)

She smiles and kisses him lightly on the lips

Francine It was lucky for both of us.

*Throughout the following, Michael will move across so that he is
standing near the intercom*

Michael Anyway — what was there to go back for?
Polly You don't miss it then?
Michael London? Not any more.
Francine Not since Sky Television. Now he can lie here and watch
West Ham and *EastEnders* and it's like you haven't really moved,
isn't it, darling?
Michael (*grinning*) That's my girl. (*He flops into the reclining chair,
putting his feet up*)
Polly Will you ever go back, d'you think?
Francine No. He won't.

This moment

Brenda What about family?

Michael knocks back his whisky and looks directly at her

Michael How's that, Brenda?
Brenda Seeing your family.
Michael My family comes out here.
Brenda Do they?
Ray The grandchildren was out here only Easter, wasn't they, Mickey?
Brenda The children, not grandchildren.

Michael gets up and pours himself more whisky as:

Michael (*"lightly"*) You been gossiping over the garden fence, have
you, Bren?
Brenda People talk.

Michael Tell me about it.

Brenda It's not an official secret, is it?

Francine Absolutely right, Brenda.   Michael's children and I don't exactly "get on".   Sad, but not unusual in our situation I would have thought.

Michael Their mother ... me getting married again so soon.

Francine I've *tried*, God alone knows I've tried.

Michael No no babe, you've done everything ... everything.   It'll sort itself out, these things always do.   And if it don't ... (*He shrugs — so that's life*)

But it's an awkward little moment that Ray attempts to deflect with:

Ray Have you seen the size of their television, Bren?

Brenda Where is it? Oh *there* it is.

Michael I bought the telly first and had the house built around it. (*He winks at Ray and moves away*)

Francine Darling, it's hideous.

Michael She indulges me.

Francine I had a moment of weakness.

Brenda Just the one?

The buzzer sounds

Michael Oh Christ. (*Into intercom*) Hallo? Hallo?

Francine This really isn't funny, you know.

Michael No, it bloody isn't.

And Michael's already pulling keys from his pocket and moving to a cupboard that he will open to reveal a small safe that he will open as:

Francine We really do have to put a stop to all this — every week, it's ... what are you doing?

Michael They want some fun, they can have some fun. (*And he straightens up and we see that he is holding a handgun*)

Ray Christ Mickey.

Francine You can't go out there with that.

Michael I'm just gonna frighten 'em, all right babe, I'm just gonna frighten 'em,

Francine We don't know who it is.

Michael It's those kids.

Francine What if it isn't?

Michael Waddaya mean, babe, what if it isn't?

Francine Mickey.

Michael It's those kids. I don't put a stop to it, they'll be at it all night. (*He moves to the terrace*)

Ray I'll come with you, eh?

Michael No need.

Ray Yeah but …

Michael No no Raymond, you stay here and entertain the ladies. (*To Francine*) If they do it again try and keep them talking.

He goes out on to the terrace and out of sight

Francine God, I hate it when he drinks whisky, he gets so … silly.

Ray Yeah, he was never very clever with the hard stuff.

Polly It's a real gun, is it?

Francine It's all right, Polly, he'll just … oh God why does he do it? (*She remains looking at the VDU*)

Ray I should go and see what's happening.

Brenda You stay where you are.

Ray Yeah but I can't just ——

Brenda This is none of your business, stay where you are.

Ray Bren ——

Francine No she's right, it'll only make things worse … (*Into the intercom*) There's no-one there, Michael — come back — please.

Brenda (*to Ray*) What's he doing with a gun?

Ray I dunno sweetheart I dunno.

Francine He's coming back, thank God for that.

Brenda (*to her*) What's he doing with a *gun*?

Francine The times I've asked him the same question.

Brenda And what's his answer?

Francine Can you believe it "added security".

Brenda That's not security, that's stupidity.

Francine A place like this — on its own, away from the town. A lot of people out here have them, whether they should or not.

Brenda Yeah but a man in his position, that's just asking for ——

There is the sudden sound of a gunshot

Ray Jesus Christ!

And a second shot — which seems to paralyse them for a moment and then Ray is moving quickly to the terrace

Brenda Keep out of it, Ray!

Ray Stay here — all of you — stay here.

And he goes out of sight

The three women remain where they are. Polly is now standing

Francine (*under her breath*) Oh my God oh my God.
Polly Phone the police.
Francine (*stunned*) What?
Brenda Phone the police.

But before any of them can move, Ray and Michael appear on the terrace

Ray is supporting Michael who is hunched forward, his gun hand hanging loosely down at his side, his other hand to his chest. He raises his head slowly and looks at them as though in shock ... and then moves his hand to reveal that it and the shirt beneath are covered in blood. Clutching his chest, he staggers in and falls as though dead. Brenda moves to him, Francine turns her head away in horror ... and then Michael is rolling over and grinning up at them with:

Michael Good? Good?
Francine You bastard ... you bastard.
Michael Just a little wind-up, girls.
Brenda Were you in on this?
Ray I knew he was up to *something*, yeah.
Brenda And you think that's funny, do you — scaring me, scaring all of us?
Ray Mickey just thought it would be a bit of a laugh.
Brenda And you went along with him — that's wonderful, wonderful.
Michael (*"licking" his bloody hand*) Mm, yummy, tomato ketchup, my favourite.
Brenda You idiots, you pair of bloody idiots.
Michael Come on, Bren, it was just a little wind-up — for Polly.
Francine Oh, for Polly, was it?
Michael Yeah, a little performance, a little bitta showbiz — (*pointing the gun at the wall*) bang!
Francine Put that stupid thing away.

Michael grins and will return the handgun to the safe as:

Ray There was no-one outside, you see.
Francine (*flat*) Oh really?
Ray He was ringing the bell himself.
Michael Did you enjoy that, Polly, did you?
Polly Yes it was uh very convincing.

Michael You see?

Brenda Very clever, yeah, very clever.

Michael Stone me, ladies, just a bitova giggle.

Brenda Oh yeah, a right giggle, I thought I'd never stop.

Francine Go and change your shirt, you look disgusting.

Michael I will, I will.

Grinning, pleased with himself, he goes upstairs

Brenda Waving a stupid bloody gun about.

Ray It had blanks in.

Brenda Like a coupla school kids. You're sixty-five years old for chrissake.

Ray It was just a bitova laugh, sweetheart.

Brenda (*to Polly*) You want a little story, Polly — here's a little story for you — one night we were all at one of these famous parties of Mickey's when he suddenly announces ——

Ray Sweetheart …

Brenda —he suddenly announces "All the chaps will now walk across the common." So out they go like a loada sheep and he says "in a straight line" and he leads off and that's exactly what they do, they walk in a straight line across Wimbledon common … through bramble bushes, through a pond, you name it, if it was in front of them you walked through it, didn't you?

Ray (*all he can come up with*) The state of us when we got back.

Brenda He claps his hands, they jump.

Francine They didn't have to jump, did they Brenda?

Brenda No they didn't, Francine.

Francine Well then.

Ray Listen. We made a mistake. We thought it would be a bitta fun for Polly.

Brenda We?

Ray You know what I mean, sweetheart.

Brenda Why don't you just for once in your life … (*She doesn't finish but instead gives a distasteful little shake of the head and waves the thought away*)

Francine Why doesn't he what, Brenda?

Brenda looks at her

Brenda Why doesn't he mind his own business, Francine.

There is an awkward little moment, broken by Michael coming down the stairs, buttoning on a fresh shirt

Michael We still in the doghouse, Raymond?

Ray I think we are, Mickey, yes.

Michael Quite right, ladies, very poor taste.

Francine Why don't we just — forget about it.

Michael Absolutely — *mea culpa* and him an 'all. Now then Polly …
this film of yours … I've been having a few thoughts about it — may
I?

Polly Well if — you know … (*She indicates – "if no-one else minds"*)

Michael (*generally*) May I?

Francine Just get on with it, will you darling?

Michael (*to Ray*) Guess who'll be sleeping in the spare room tonight?

Francine Just — get on with it.

Michael You see … it occurs to me … that what you've got … is too
straightforward. So I thought to myself … what we need … is an
angle. I said it to *you*, didn't I, Ray?

Ray He did: what we need is an angle he said.

Michael And the angle I came up with is this: we do it as a series of
flashbacks. Told through the eyes of the chaps as they are today. The
men they have become. So in terms of casting — and we all know
the importance of casting, don't we, we all know where the money is
— you can have your Gary Oldmans and your Ray Winstones as they
were … and the likes of your Robert de Niros, your Gene Hackmans
as we — they — are now.

Ray Your Michael Caines.

Michael Good one, Raymond.

Ray *Get Carter*. The best.

Michael We've got it on DVD, haven't we babe?

Francine Have we, I've no idea.

Michael Anyway, faces like that.

Ray That Indian bloke, Ben something.

Polly Kingsley.

Ray That's him – Gandhi.

Michael And if you *do* go for the flashback approach, it will also allow
you your McGuffin. McGuffin — the term believed to be originated
by Alfred Hitchcock — being an object around which a plot is built.
Oh yes Polly … I know all about that sorta stuff. Well I've had so
much (*he would have said "crap" but changes it to*), rubbish shown to
me, I thought to myself I can write better than this stuff and Francine
said, and quite rightly … what was it you said babe?

Francine I've forgotten.

Michael No you haven't, no you haven't … she said … "if you're
gonna do something you've got to have a platform from which you
can speak with authority" …

Brenda I can hear you saying it, Francine …

Michael So I sent away for all the books and stuff, all your William Goldbergs ——

Francine Man, Gold*man* …

Michael — Gold*man* and that one who done the lectures — Robert McGee, that's him innit babe?

Francine Near enough.

Michael Robert McGee etcetera — which is how I come across the McGuffin principle — which in our film I thought could be a little gold crucifix the character based on Harry Harmon is always playing with. Every time we see him, he's playing with this little gold crucifix. So we get the visual link from the old man to the young man and vice versa.

Brenda Harry was Jewish.

Michael So?

Brenda So he wouldn't be playing with a crucifix, he'd be playing with a salt beef sandwich.

Michael All right, so he's playing with a salt beef sandwich — but you take my point, Polly?

Polly I do — yes.

Michael Worth taking on board would you say?

Polly I mean like — yes. Great.

Michael Good. Good to be of service.

There is the distant sound of fireworks

Hallo — sounds like the fireworks have started. (*He moves to look out over the terrace as:*)

Francine They do like their fireworks — now then — who needs topping up? (*She will top up Polly and Brenda's glasses as:*)

Michael Tell you what, Polly: why don't you and Raymond meet up when you get back to London — he can introduce you to some of the chaps — the *real* chaps.

Polly Well — yes — that would be — fantastic.

Michael There y'go.

Polly If it wouldn't be — you know.

Ray No — you know — whatever you fancy.

Michael I mean officially — I mean on the payroll.

Polly Oh I'm sure I can arrange something.

Michael Some nice little exes, eh Raymondo? (*He rubs his thumb and finger together*)

Ray Well … we can talk about that later.

Brenda Just make sure you do.

Michael Raymond can be very very useful.

Ray I'll try, course I will.

Michael Have you read any of his little books, Polly? As part of your research?

Polly I've got a whole pile to read actually — like, you know, everybody's.

Michael Oh you've gotta read Raymond's….he does these little books — *A Beginner's Guide to the London Underworld* — that sort of stuff. When I say he does them, this other bloke writes 'em and Raymond does a little watchacallit, that bit at the front.

Polly Foreword.

Michael Foreword, that's it. (*He pours himself another whisky as:*) He takes it very seriously, don't you, Raymond?

Ray Yeah, well, it's a …

Michael It's a business — right. He's got himself a website, Polly, you should have a look at it.

Polly I will.

Michael Then there's his coach tours of course. He does these coach tours round the East End, showing people where Frankie done this, Ronnie done that and they love it, don't they, Raymond, they love it.

Ray (*quietly, trying to make light of it*) Leave it out, Mickey.

Michael See, what I've never understood is … what exactly do you do?

Brenda What d'you mean, what does he do, you've just *said*.

Michael I mean you stand at the front, do you, with a microphone, pointing outa the window?

Ray Yeah, well, something like that.

Michael Then what — you go round with the hat?

Francine Who's for some coffee?

General ad-libbing of no thanks

Michael You see the thing is ——

Francine Change the subject, darling.

Michael Change the subject — what does *that* mean?

Francine It means you're getting drunk and you're getting silly.

Michael I'm *interested* — so are you, aren't you, Polly — it's why she's here — and Raymond don't mind, do you Raymond?

Ray No, I don't mind.

Michael Course he don't mind. Nothing to be ashamed of.

Brenda What's there to be ashamed of?

Michael What I just said.

Brenda Was it?

Michael It's business — right, Ray?

Ray It's something that was put to me. By this bloke I met, this
producer.
Brenda You don't have to explain.
Ray I don't do it all the time, just now and again. That's all, just now
and again.
Michael Like I said — business. Giving the punters what they want.
Although I have to tell you that when I first heard … well frankly it
made me a bit upset. I mean … it's not very dignified, is it? I mean,
if you wanted a few bob … you could have asked *me*. Let's face it, it
wouldn't be the first time. And happy to oblige.

This moment. The sound of the distant fireworks

Polly I will have a coffee if I may.
Francine Of course you may. Anyone else?

Brenda and Ray ad lib no thanks

Francine Tea?
Ray Yeah *I* wouldn't mind a cuppa tea, thank you Francine.
Francine Ordinary or Earl Grey?
Ray Er — ordinary.
Brenda Have you got any camomile?
Francine I think I have — yes.
Brenda He'll have camomile.
Francine One coffee one camomile tea. (*She smiles*)

Francine goes through into the kitchen

Polly Then I suppose I should go.
Michael Got a date, have you, Polly?
Polly No I just thought ——
Michael Well there you go then. Besides. We haven't finished. Have
we? (*Said with a smile but making it clear that she goes when he says
she goes*)

*Michael will unnecessarily top up her glass, make to refill Brenda's but
she stops him*

How are you with the water, Raymond? Oh no, you're having camomile tea, aren't you?
Brenda It helps him sleep.

Michael is pouring himself a whisky

Michael This is the stuff to help you sleep. A nice single malt. They haven't got much right, the jocks, but they cracked it with this stuff. Nectar. She's quite right though: I do get drunk easy. Fellas used to say to me gor blimey why aren't you a woman, cheapest ... dunno what it is. Coupla drinks and it goes straight to my head but I do, I enjoy it. One of my little weaknesses. And yeah I get lairy, I admit it, I do get lairy. Always did, didn't I, Ray?

Ray You did, yeah.

Michael And who was always there to look after me? My friend Raymond. (*He kisses the top of Raymond's head*) So then Polly: what else can we tell you?

Polly Well, um ... as *you're* here — Brenda — I just wondered — you know like — being the wife of — you know ...

Brenda No. No I don't know. (*She does of course*)

Polly I mean it must be — difficult.

Ray No offence Polly but I'm not sure I'm happy about this.

Brenda You mean did I know he was at it.

Ray Now now Bren ...

Brenda It's all right, I've got nothing to hide.

Michael Course she's got nothing to hide. You speak your mind, Bren — say what you think.

Ray Excuse me, Mickey, this is between me and Brenda.

Michael raises his hands in mock-surrender

Brenda That's what you want to know, isn't it Polly ... did I know he was at it?

Slight pause

Polly Yes.

Brenda As long as I didn't know exactly what he was up to, I didn't ask questions.

Polly But you must have known how he — made his money.

Brenda What he didn't want me to know, I didn't ask.

Polly I don't understand that.

Brenda I don't suppose you do, no.

Ray Brenda ...

Brenda It's all right, it's all right.

Polly I mean I don't want to sound judgemental but ... God, I don't know how to say this ... but I mean ... you must have known ... I mean the truth is you must have ... you must have known that you were like living off crime. And violence.

Brenda I said. What I didn't know I didn't ask about.

Polly And what about — well — when he was in prison.
Brenda I waited for him to come out.
Polly No I mean …
Brenda Do you get angry? Do you get upset? What do you think? You cope, you get on with it.
Michael With a little bit of help from your friends.

Brenda looks at him and:

Brenda Yes. We mustn't forget *that*, must we?
Polly You see …
Brenda Yeah it's hard for you to understand, I appreciate that, Polly. The thing is, you see … women like me don't have none of your middle class anxieties.   Like shame. Or guilt. I'm sure you can understand *that*. It's your sorta language. Should be — it came outa your sorta book. My daughter read it to me. Deborah, my youngest. (*To Michael*) *You* know, Mickey: the educated one. The one you paid to put through college.
Michael No need to mention that, Brenda.
Brenda Just thought I'd get in first, that's all.

This moment and Michael grins and:

Michael You can see why he loves her, eh Polly?
Brenda More to the point, I love him. I've loved him from when I was fifteen years old. I've loved him, good and bad, ever since.   Mind you … I won't do if I ever catch him with a fag in his mouth.

Francine comes in with a small tray bearing two mugs of coffee, one of tea, milk and sugar

Francine Here we go… (*She gives a coffee to Polly, the tea to Ray, and the second coffee to Michael*)

Polly and Ray ad lib their thanks as:

Michael What's this?
Francine It's called black coffee, darling — it'll do you good. More to the point it'll do *us* good — how about you, Polly — cream or milk?
Polly Oh umm … milk I think.

Francine will pass the milk jug and Ray will fiddle the teabag out of his mug, not quite sure where to put it as:

Brenda The one you should be talking to, Polly, is Francine.

Francine Oh yes, about what?

Brenda Now that's much more interesting — wouldn't you say, Mickey?

Ray Francine doesn't know nothing about it.

Brenda That right, is it Francine?

Francine I'm sorry, I seem to have missed out on something.

Michael Brenda being a bit naughty, babe.

Brenda You ask *me* — *his* wife. Why not Francine? His?

Michael Because it's different, that's why.

Brenda You mean she's now and not then.

Michael Exactly.

Brenda I still think it's a question Polly might like answering. Yes?

Polly Well — yes.

Francine What question?

Brenda Speak your mind, Francine. Say what you think.

Francine Well perhaps if I …

Ray This is not the time, Bren.

Brenda How could someone like you marry a criminal?

Michael Retired criminal.

Brenda *Retired* criminal.

Francine Someone like me.

Brenda Someone like you, someone like him.

This moment

Francine I knew nothing about Michael's past when I met him.

Brenda It wasn't the attraction.

Ray Leave it out sweetheart.

Francine Attraction?

Brenda Some women find it attractive.

Francine Is that right?

Brenda So I'm told.

Francine And you think I'm one of them. Perhaps you're right — perhaps you're my bit of rough, darling.

Michael Charming.

Francine That's what you mean, isn't it, Brenda?

Brenda Takes all sorts.

Ray Come on girls …

Francine There were rumours. I was interested in the man, not the rumours.

Brenda There we are then, Polly: two of a kind.

Francine With all due respect …

Brenda Just the one difference though.

Francine What's that?

Brenda One of us has had all the benefits without having had to serve any of the time.

This moment

Throughout the following, Ray will start to have little coughing fits. Quietly, but getting increasingly insistent. Brenda will pass a handkerchief to him and he will cover his mouth as he coughs

Francine Again — you're absolutely right. However … if, in some way, you feel I should — apologize …

Brenda No, no. Just — making it clear. For Polly.

Francine Oh of course — for Polly.

Polly I umm I mean — you know.

Francine Then let's make sure we *are* clear: if I thought for one moment that Michael was still — "active" as he calls it — I would have had nothing to do with him. Nothing.

Said for whose benefit — Polly's, Brenda's — or Michael's? This moment and:

Michael You know what *I* think, Brenda? I think you're well out of order.

Ray She didn't mean it in a *nasty* way, did you Bren?

Michael However … however … she has a point. This woman is an angel. I will never cease to be amazed at how someone like her … could take on someone … like me.

Francine Well just you remember that, darling.

Michael (*hand on heart*) I will never forget.

Francine Yes well we'll see about that — now then are we going to watch these fireworks or aren't we?

Ray Actually … I was thinking of getting an early night.

Michael Polly hasn't finished with her questions.

Ray Well — tomorrow maybe.

Michael She won't be here tomorrow.

Brenda He can see Polly in London.

Francine Yes, go to bed if you want to, Ray, you look tired.

Ray Be in touch then, eh Polly?

Michael *I've* gotta coupla questions as it happens.

Francine Tomorrow.

Michael Two minutes.

Ray Me, you mean?

Michael Gotta say it, Raymond, get it off me chest — you know what I mean?

Ray No.

Michael That book, wassisname's book, the one we were talking about earlier.

Ray Oh yeah?

Michael You get some very nice mentions.

Ray You said you hadn't read it.

Michael Yeah, I did, didn't I?

Ray I'm not with you.

Michael How you did this ... how you did that ... seems to me there's not enough hours in the day for all the villainy you're supposed to have masterminded.

Francine Do we have to?

Brenda Go to bed, Ray.

Ray You know how it is, Mickey.

Michael You exaggerate.

Ray Course.

Michael Yeah well that's the game, that I can understand. What I cannot understand is someone crossing the line, especially when they do it at my expense.

Ray What are you saying, Mickey?

Michael Blowing your horn a bit, weren't you, Raymond? Read his lousy book you'd think it was you running the firm not me.

Ray That's the way he put it down, you know what they're like, they twist things.

Michael So why didn't you correct him?

Ray Bloody hell, Mickey, half a page. (*He is becoming somewhat breathless with the coughing*)

Michael Half a page, half a sentence, it makes me look small.

Ray No.

Michael Look — small.

Ray No one was trying to make you look small.

Michael But you did, Raymond, you did. That's what some people do, you see, Polly — they puff themselves up by trying to make other people look small.

Brenda I don't believe I'm hearing this.

Ray Yeah, what's this all about, Mickey?

Michael It's about me having the hump, *that's* what it's about

Francine It's about you having too much to drink. Come on, Polly, let's go and watch the fireworks.

Michael Stay where you are, Polly.

Brenda She doesn't need to hear any of this.
Michael Stay where you are. (*Said quietly but with unquestionable authority*)

This moment

Ray One question.
Michael Hello, he's asking a question.
Ray Why say you hadn't read it?
Michael Because I was trying to avoid it coming to *this*, that's why.
Brenda So why didn't you try a bit harder?
Ray (*making light of it*) He's winding me up.
Michael Did you say something, Brenda love?
Ray He is, he's winding me up.
Michael Let the woman speak — she's been dying to have a pop at me ever since you got here.
Ray Leave it out, Mick.
Michael Am I right or am I right, Brenda my love?
Francine I really think we should talk about something else.
Ray Why would she have a pop at you?
Brenda I can speak for myself, thank you.
Michael Who knows? But there's *something* on your mind — *I* know it, *you* know it...
Brenda Like what?
Michael Like maybe you should — give it an airing.
Brenda You're drunk.
Michael I'm with friends, I'm entitled. That's a nasty cough you've got there, Raymond.
Ray I think I'll just ... get some air.

He goes through into the garden, coughing, as:

Brenda (*calling*) Have you got your puffer?

Ray holds up a hand indicating "yes", and goes out of sight

Michael Puffer?
Brenda He has trouble breathing sometimes.
Francine Will he be all right?
Brenda He'll be all right. (*Nevertheless she will move to look out over the terrace as:*)
Michael Raymond? Course he will, made a stone.

Unseen by the others, Francine gives Michael a look, bordering on the angry. He makes a small placatory gesture to her and:

Michael All right, Polly — enjoying yourself?
Polly Fine. Thank you.
Michael Anything you want, just …
Polly Thank you.

He smiles. She tries one back. A moment. Brenda returns to sit

Michael How long have we known each other, Brenda?
Brenda (*to Polly*) Since I was at school and he was avoiding National Service. (*To Michael*) *That* long.
Michael So you owe it to me.
Brenda To what?
Michael To say what's on your mind.
Brenda What do *you* think I've got on my mind?
Michael I dunno: that's why I'm asking.

Francine sighs heavily

Brenda What do you want to hear? I'm jealous?
Francine You're at the *La Perla*, aren't you, Polly?
Michael Jealous.
Polly Yes.
Brenda Satisfied?
Francine How are you finding it?
Polly It's very good.
Michael Jealous … because I've got … (*considering, then making a sweeping gesture with:*) this … and you've got … what *have* you got? You've got Raymond, you've got three wonderful kids, you've got a very nice little house in New Barnet …
Brenda That's what I've got — yes.
Michael So maybe you don't think it's enough. Maybe all these years you've been thinking you've got second prize.
Brenda Drunk or sober, Mickey … you're a cunt.

This moment. Then Francine gets up and pours herself a drink. Michael "smiles" and:

   Why are we here, Mickey?
Michael Ah! Ah!
Brenda Why are we here?

Michael You're my guests.
Brenda Two years, not a word.
Michael I'm making up for it.
Brenda You want something.
Michael (*amused*) I what?
Brenda You want something.

Ray appears on the terrace, dabbing his mouth, unseen by the others as:

Michael Well that makes a nice change, eh Bren? Usually it's you doing the wanting and me doing the giving.
Brenda We've never asked you for anything.
Michael Not — in so many words — no.
Ray (*coming in*) What's this?
Brenda Are you all right?
Ray No no — what he just said — you think we're on the take?
Brenda It's him who's on the take.
Michael Oh yes?
Brenda You always were, you always will be.
Francine (*sighing heavily*) I really don't think Polly ——
Michael She's being educated — right, Polly?
Polly Actually, I was wondering where the umm …
Brenda All right with *you*, Mickey? The girl wants to use the toilet.
Francine There's one by the door, or upstairs … (*To Michael*) I just knew this would happen, I knew it.

Polly moves to the door, but changes her mind and goes upstairs

Ray (*quietly*) We never once asked you for a handout, Mickey. What you gave you gave — and we appreciated.
Michael (*with an expansive gesture*) Which is all I'm saying.
Ray We know that, Mickey.
Michael So?
Brenda So money is easy. It's giving from *here* that counts.
Francine Meaning what?
Brenda You mean you haven't found out yet?
Francine Found out what?
Brenda That he has to have control ——
Ray Bren …
Brenda — he has to be in charge, has to be number one. It's like a packa chimpanzees, you're the king of the heap and everyone else has to get into line.

Michael That David Attenborough's got a lot to answer for, eh babe?

Brenda Everywhere we went it was you you you … you and your big fat Gucci wallet … Mr Big … somebody gets married, somebody gets christened, somebody gets buried and it's you you you lobbing out the money and the cigars … your own kids can't stand the sight of you … they hate the way you interfere all the time, chucking your money around … you haven't got a heart, Mickey, not a real heart, you've got a control button and you know what it does? It destroys people, it takes away pride — your own wife *died* because of you — and this man … I've watched this man grow small because of you and I tell you — the best present you ever gave us was coming out here, giving us and everyone else a chance to breathe.

This moment. Ray is looking down at the floor, unable to make eye contact

Michael Waddaya mean, my wife died because of me?

Brenda Didn't she?

Francine She was in a car accident.

Brenda She was full of valium, getting away from *him*. The poor cow probably didn't know what she was doing.

Michael You know, do you?

Brenda She used to write to me. Sometimes she even plucked up courage enough to phone.

This moment. And Michael chooses to make light of it with:

Michael You don't change, eh Bren? Still cleaning your teeth with vinegar.

Francine I think an apology's in order, don't you?

Ray Listen … we've all had a bit too much to drink …

Michael No no no, it's all very interesting and you know what, Raymond? You're the only one who hasn't said his piece.

Ray Come on Mickey.

Michael Made you grow small? What's all that about, made you grow small … I didn't make you *anything* — God done that.

This moment

Ray (*quietly*) Yeah, well, OK Mickey.

Michael (*smiling*) Looks like it's just you and me, Bren. Raymond, as ever, is making no contribution.

Brenda I despise you, Mickey. I always have.

Michael No sleep for *me* tonight, babe.

Brenda I can't remember a time when you weren't trying to put him down and he just stands there and takes it.

Ray Bren ...

Brenda You do. Look at you now.

Michael Maybe he knows which side his bread is buttered.

Brenda How about *this* for her film...this Mr Big, this Mr Knowall who continually ridicules a man, tries to make a man look small and why? Ask him why, Francine.

Francine I don't think so.

Brenda Because maybe in his heart he knew he couldn't do without him. Well it's you who looks small, Mickey. Not him.

Michael D'you know, Raymond, it's like you're not here.

Ray (*quietly*) Don't ... just don't go too far, eh Mickey?

Michael What will you do, Raymond, hit me? Put your hankie away and take a poke at me? That's your answer to everything, isn't it — or was — I can't speak for you *now*, but looking at the state of you I'd say you'd be pushing it a bit squaring up to Francine here. Polly! Where is she?

Francine Keeping out of it if she's got any sense.

Michael I got another idea for her film an'all ... How about this character who agrees with everything everybody says, a yes-man who gets on everybody's fucking tits. (*To Brenda*) Now look what you've made me do, you've made me swear in front of my wife. You see, babe, villainy is no different than anything else. You've got your main man and you've got your hangers-on, your nobodies and they suck off you like those mosquitoes out there. (*Back to Brenda with a change of tone*) The only thing I've ever asked of *him* is loyalty.

Brenda Loyalty? You don't know the first thing about loyalty ... loyalty means only one thing to you.

Michael And what's that?

Brenda Total fucking obedience.

Ray (*quietly*) All right Bren ...

Brenda Loyalty works both ways. But not with you.

Michael I've given this man ——

Ray Waddaya mean "this man"? It's me. Me.

This moment

Why didn't you invite us to your wedding, Mickey?

Francine That was my fault, he was devastated.

Ray You didn't want us here, did you? You lied about it and you knew I'd find out but you thought I'd swallow it like I've swallowed everything else and I would have, wouldn't I? I would have. Because that's *me*, innit?

Brenda (*softly*) It *isn't* you. Only with *him*.

Ray You think I don't know, Mickey? I'm nothing in your eyes. I sit here listening to you going on about your grandchildren — do you once ask me about mine? My kids, my family? You get some silly little girl round here and you can't resist trying to put me down in front of her ... "Waddaya do, stand up at the front with a microphone, pointing outa the window?" ... Yeah, that's about it, Mickey, I *do*. Loyalty, obedience, duty, respect ... that's what royalty expect of their butler, innit? And that's you, Mickey. That's how you see yourself.

Michael Go to bed, you're beginning to make yourself look silly.

Brenda Come on.

Ray I haven't finished. Me. I haven't finished.

Michael Me? I have. (*He knocks back his whisky, bangs down the glass and makes to go*)

Ray blocks Michael's path

Oh yes?

Ray She's right. I have let you walk all over me and you know why? Because all these years I've seen you as more than a friend, Mickey, to me you've been like family and family you put up with things, because you love 'em.

Michael Oh dear oh dear.

Ray Yeah, that's funny, innit.

Michael I think it's quite sad.

Ray There's nothing I wouldn't have done for you, Mickey.

Michael Move.

Ray And I've always kidded myself that come the big one you'd do the same.

Michael Move.

Ray And I'm *still* doing it, d'you know that? I'm *still* looking after you. I'm still looking after you.

This moment

Michael Meaning what?

This moment. Then Ray shakes his head slightly and moves away. This moment. The distant sound of the fireworks — bigger fireworks — and people cheering

Leave us alone for a minute, will you ladies? Please.

This moment. Then Francine goes out on to the terrace

Ray (*softly*) Please, Bren.

This moment. Then Brenda goes outside on to the terrace

Michael waits for the women to move out of sight and moves to apparently pour himself a scotch but in fact — and unseen by Raymond or us — to activate the DVD recorder set near the television

Michael (*quietly*) Meaning what?
Ray I thought that's why you got me out here, I thought you wanted to talk about it. (*A moment*) Merrison called me. He wanted to mark my card. They're re-opening the Tony Manzi business.
Michael So everyone keeps telling me.
Ray They know now for certain he was topped. They've got the bullets.

This moment

Michael Siddown.

Ray sits

So they know he was topped …
Ray They're going for *you*, Mickey.
Michael They're what?
Ray They want *you*.
Michael Then they're gonna be unlucky, aren't they?
Ray They've found someone they think they can persuade to put you in.
Michael Who?
Ray Johnny Edmonds.
Michael Fuckin' Johnny Edmonds?
Ray He's up for a big one. Merrison reckons they can do a deal.
Michael Yeah, yeah, I get the picture. Know where he is, do you?

This moment. Then Ray nods

I'll have a word with him. Point out the error of his ways.
Ray I've already *had* a word with him.

This moment

Michael will get up and move to stand behind Ray during:

Michael Still looking after me, eh Raymond? All that shit you come out with and you're right, you're still looking after me. I'm touched. I am, I'm touched. (*He pats Ray's cheek*)

Nothing from Ray

I'll see you're all right.
Ray I don't want your money, Mickey.
Michael Suit yourself.
Ray I want you to stick to your story that I was with you the night Manzi got done.

This moment

Michael Are you saying …
Ray Yeah, that's what I'm saying.
Michael You put him down — you put Tony Manzi down?
Ray I had to, Mickey ——
Michael You fuckin' put him down ——
Ray — he was mouthing off, it got out of hand. (*He pulls out his cigarettes*)
Michael I told you not to go near him — and put the fuckin' fags away.
Ray He would have caused you a lotta grief, Mickey.
Michael You stupid fuckin' — you coulda caused me a fuckin' bucket-loada grief, I ought to … (*He makes an effort to calm down, to think about it*) So.   You put him down, because of me, but without me knowing anything about it. I have got that right, haven't I?
Ray Yeah.
Michael I knew nothing about it.
Ray You knew nothing about it.
Michael Why didn't you tell me afterwards?
Ray I didn't want you to have to think about it.
Michael You what?
Ray I didn't want you to have to think about it. Cheryl getting ill and everything.

Michael looks at him and almost laughs

Michael You cunt … You stupid fuckin' … From now on, keep your mouth shut, leave it to me.

Ray Yeah.
Michael Now bugger off and smoke your fag.

This moment

Bugger off, Raymond.

This moment. And Raymond goes on to the terrace, pulling out his cigarettes. He stops for a moment, his back to us, coughing, then moves slowly away and out of sight

Michael remains standing where he was. Then he moves and ejects a disc from the machine. He looks at it. Frankly, he despises himself

During this, Polly comes down the stairs

He looks at her. This moment and:

Polly Well?
Michael It's all here — take it. (*He holds out the disc to her. He is quite a different Michael now — no hint of drunkenness*)

And it's quite a different Polly: assertive, controlled. She takes her time about taking the disc from him

Polly I do hope you pressed all the right buttons.
Michael Just take it, will you?

She smiles, puts the disc into her rucksack

What happens now?
Polly We put it all together and give him a pull.
Michael And you keep me out of it.
Polly That was the deal.
Michael You tell Merrison I don't want any more contact with him.
Polly Trust me.

This moment. Is she mocking him?

Michael You've got what you wanted — bugger off.
Polly I've been invited to watch the fireworks — besides — I'd like a drink — a proper drink — some of your single malt – the real stuff, not that watered down rubbish you've been drinking — and no ice.

A moment. Then he pours her a glass of whisky, gives her the glass, takes up his own. She remains facing him, close, and raises her glass

> *Throughout this, Francine — unseen by them — will appear on the terrace. She stops on seeing them close together*

Polly Here's to a result then. (*She raises her glass*)
Michael Drink it and bugger off.
Polly Nice. (*She smiles, remains where she is, takes a mouthful of whisky*)

And Michael becomes aware of Francine

Francine How very cosy.
Michael It's all right, babe, it's all right.
Francine What's going on?
Michael Nothing's going on, nothing.
Polly Absolutely.   Sorry and all that but he's far too old for me, I promise you.

This moment

Francine (*quietly*) I'll ask you again: what's going on?
Polly I'd better introduce myself properly — Detective Sergeant Phillips, Serious Crime Squad. I'm sorry, I haven't got my card but Mickey will no doubt vouch for me.
Francine (*to Michael*) Are you in trouble?
Michael No.
Francine Because if you've been lying to me …
Michael Nothing like that, babe, I swear. (*He moves to look out over the terrace*)
Polly Eight years ago an associate of your husband's — a man named Anthony Manzi — went missing, believed dead. Last month his body turned up. He'd been shot in the head and chest. A criminal named John Edmonds is prepared to say that your husband either killed or ordered the killing of Mr Manzi.
Michael He's a nothing, babe, a nobody.
Polly A retired officer named Merrison advised your husband that the case had been re-opened. He came to us and we — worked out a deal.
Francine What — deal?
Michael Raymond did Manzi — I had nothing to do with it.
Francine Raymond?

Polly Your husband got a confession — a recorded confession out of him. That's what today has been all about. Isn't it, Mickey?

Michael I knew he wouldn't say anything unless I — pushed him into it.

Francine Are you saying that's why you got him here?

He can't bring himself to answer

Are you saying …

Michael *Yes.*

Francine This whole thing has been a …

Polly A performance — yes. Mickey prides himself on his ability to — perform — don't you, Mickey?

Francine And you told me nothing.

Michael I didn't want to involve you …

Francine You lied to me …

Michael No babe …

Francine You swore to me you'd keep your hands clean..

Michael That's why I did it, babe, that's what this is all about … I wouldn't do it to him otherwise … for Chrissake, they would have had me outa here — all right it woulda taken time but I know these people, they would have *had* me and I couldn't risk that, I couldn't risk losing *you.*

Polly So. It was either his old friend Raymond or the woman he loves. No contest.

Brenda comes in from the terrace. She stops, sensing the atmosphere. Then:

Brenda If you're coming outside you'll need a pullover, it's getting chilly.

Francine (*graciously*) Thank you.

A moment. Then Brenda moves past them and goes upstairs. They wait until she is out of sight and:

(*to Michael*) There'll be no comeback.

Michael None.

Francine What if he finds out?

Polly He won't.

Francine You can't guarantee that.

Polly We can. And you're forgetting Raymond. It wouldn't be the first time he's taken the heat for good old Mickey, eh Mickey?

Michael You've got what you wanted. Just piss off, will you?
Polly What *I* wanted?
Francine Go and see if he's all right.
Michael Babe …
Francine Go and see if he's all right.

This moment. Then Michael goes out on to the terrace and out of sight

We've got a good life here. I won't have it destroyed.
Polly It won't *be* destroyed. Not unless your husband has a sudden fit of morality — which I very much doubt, don't you?
Francine You will lock the gates after you.
Polly I haven't finished my drink.
Francine As soon as you have then.
Polly Of course I'll lock the gates. We don't want any undesirables getting into your lovely home, do we?

This moment. Then Francine gives her icy smile and moves to the terrace and out of sight

As soon as she's gone, Polly knocks back her drink and takes up her rucksack. She puts the script into it. At the same time, although we can't see it, she is putting a disc into a recorder in her rucksack

As she does, Brenda is coming downstairs wearing a cardigan and carrying a sweater for Ray

Brenda Not watching the fireworks?
Polly It's a bit chilly for me.
Brenda (*of the sweater*) I've got another one if you …
Polly Mrs Barrett … I want to show you something.

Brenda looks at her

Brenda Oh yes?
Polly It will explain a great deal to you.
Brenda Like what?
Polly Like why you're here.

This moment

Brenda You're Old Bill, aren't you?
Polly Sit down. Please.

Brenda I don't want to sit down, I want to know what's going on.
Polly Sit down and you'll find out.

*This moment. Then Brenda sits. Compliant because she wants to find
out what is going on. Polly checks the terrace, then takes up the remote
control and activates the television. We see the split-screens, then this
room, full screen —Michael and Ray. Polly skips through from Michael's
"Meaning what?" — there is no sound — and freezes it on Michael's
"You're not up to something, are you Raymond?" and then the disc
plays, normal speed, with sound. We see now why Michael — who is
of course fully aware of the hidden camera — got Ray to sit in that
particular chair*

Michael (*on screen*) Still looking after me, eh Raymond? All that shit
you came out with and you are, you're still looking after me. I'm
touched. I am, I'm touched.

Polly fast-forwards to:

I'll see you're all right.
Ray (*on screen*) I don't want your money, Mickey.
Michael (*on screen*) Suit yourself.
Ray (*on screen*) I want you to stick to your story that I was with you the
night Manzi got done.

Forward to:

Michael You put him down — you put Tony Manzi down?
Ray (*on screen*) I had to, Mickey …
Brenda Oh Christ.

Forward to:

Michael (*on screen*) I knew nothing about it.
Ray (*on screen*) You knew nothing about it.

*The picture freezes and then reverts to the split-screen. Brenda remains
quite still as Polly — who has positioned herself so that she can keep an
eye outside — moves to eject the disc*

Brenda You can't do this. He's sixty-five years old and he's ill, more ill
than he knows. He can't go inside again, it would kill him.
Polly You're probably right. Not that it seems to worry Mickey.

Brenda Waddaya mean, worry Mickey?

Polly He's giving us Raymond.

Brenda No — no, he's pulled some strokes, but not even Mickey …

Polly I've just shown you.

Brenda What? Shown me what? What's your game, what are you after?

Polly You're right. It's not your husband we want, it's Mickey.

Brenda For Manzi? No chance.

Polly Not for Manzi …

Brenda For what? He hasn't been at it for years.

Polly You think someone like Mickey could wash his hands just like that? He's financing one of the biggest drug set-ups we've got into …

Brenda Drugs? I don't believe it.

Polly He doesn't know we're on to him yet — we're building a case but we need more.

Brenda And you think I'm gonna give it to you? Bugger off.

Polly I'm offering you a deal.

Brenda And I'm telling you to bugger off.

Polly looks at her and:

Polly I thought that you might take some persuading. This one he made for me … (*She holds up the disc*) This one he knows nothing about. (*She puts the second disc — the one from her bag — into the player and starts it, again moving so that she can see out on to the terrace. She will jump forward at various times so that we see and hear — and all from Polly's concealed camera point of view:*)

Polly (*on screen*) Well?

Michael (*on screen*) It's all here — take it. (*He holds out the first disc to her*)

Polly (*on screen*) I do hope you pressed all the right buttons.

Michael (*on screen*) Just … take it, will you?

She smiles, puts the disc into her rucksack

What happens now?

Polly (*on screen*) We put it all together and give him a pull.

Michael (*on screen*) And you keep me out of it.

Polly (*on screen*) That was the deal.

Forward to:

Francine (*on screen*) I'll ask you again: what's going on?

Polly (*on screen*) A retired officer named Merrison advised your husband that the case had been re-opened.   He came to us and we — worked out a deal.

Francine (*on screen*) What — deal?

Michael (*on screen*) Raymond did Manzi — I had nothing to do with it.

Brenda You bastard!

Polly (*on screen*) Your husband got a confession — a recorded confession out of him.   That's what today has been all about.   Isn't it, Mickey?

Michael (*on screen*) I knew he wouldn't say anything unless I — pushed him into it.

Brenda (*softly*) I'll kill him, I'll bloody kill him.

Francine (*on screen*) Are you saying that's why you got him here? Are you saying ...

Michael (*on screen*) ... yes ...

Francine (*on screen*) This whole thing has been a...

Polly (*on screen*) ... a performance — yes.   Mickey prides himself on his ability to — perform — don't you, Mickey?

Francine (*on screen*) And you told me nothing.

Michael (*on screen*) I didn't want to involve you ...

Francine (*on screen*) You lied to me ...

Michael (*on screen*) No babe ...

Francine (*on screen*) You swore to me you'd keep your hands clean..

Michael (*on screen*) That's why I did it, babe, that's what this is all about ... I wouldn't do it to him otherwise ... for Chrissake, they would have had me outa here — all right it woulda taken time but I know these people, they would have *had* me and I couldn't risk that, I couldn't risk losing *you*.

Polly (*on screen*) So.   It was either his old friend Raymond or the woman he loves.   No contest.

Polly stops the disc and removes it from the player.   Brenda has re-mained motionless.   Polly puts the two discs into her rucksack as:

Polly Not even Mickey eh?

Brenda I'll kill him.

Polly You can do better than that.

Brenda I see.   We're getting to it now, are we?

Polly As I said — we're building a case but we need more.

A moment

Brenda Go on.

Polly Once a week he goes to Gibraltar to look after his business interests. Tell him you'd like to go with him, have a look at the place. When he's there we'll give him a pull.

Brenda Why?

Polly Information received that he's carrying certain substances.

Brenda He's too clever, he wouldn't go near the stuff.

Polly When your husband came through customs ...

Brenda He was stopped — so that's what it was about — you planted something.

Polly A package was put under the bottom lining of his bag.

Brenda And I'm supposed to plant it on Mickey.

Polly When you go to Gibraltar, put it somewhere in his car.

Brenda He'll have a brief tie you in knots.

Polly Here, yes, he's got a lot of friends in the local police and they could hold up an extradition for years — long enough for him to leg it to Cyprus or wherever. That's why we want him in Gib. We can have him on a plane and out of there in a couple of hours.

Brenda If ... *if* I do this ... what happens to Ray?

Polly Nothing happens to Ray: It all gets lost.

Brenda He's admitting killing a man.

Polly The man was a gangster. Call it rough justice. Have we got a deal or haven't we?

A moment

Brenda If I do this ... I don't want Ray knowing anything about it.

Polly If he did we'd have no deal, would we? He'd rather have his tongue torn out than put his dear old pal Mickey in the frame.

Brenda And if I don't do it, you'll no doubt turn your attention back to Tony Manzi.

Polly It's an unfair world, Mrs Barrett, we'd have no alternative. Now we know what we know. It's up to you.

Brenda says nothing. Polly takes up Ray's sweater

I'll give this to your husband while you have a think about it.

Again there is nothing from Brenda

Polly goes out with the sweater

Brenda remains still. She suddenly shivers as though cold and pulls her cardigan closer. The sound of fireworks and cheering

Michael comes in, holding his glass

*Brenda doesn't respond.   He indicates his glass, miming does she want
a drink.   A moment and she gives a slight shake of the head.   He pours
himself a drink and makes to go out, but:*

Michael (*awkwardly*) Listen — er — Bren — you're absolutely right
— it wasn't just for a holiday I asked you out here.
Brenda No?
Michael I — er — I heard things weren't too good and I — er — I wanted
to — er — you know — look after you, slip you a few readies.

A moment

Brenda That's very nice of you, Mickey. But we're all right.
Michael Well — you know.
Brenda Yes.
Michael Well he is my Number One Man.
Brenda And you're his. (*She smiles*)

Which relaxes him a little

Michael You and me, eh Bren? Can't help having a go, can we?
Brenda No. No, I suppose you're right.
Michael Since we were kids, eh, just the three of us.
Brenda Yes.
Michael You know what *I* think? I think it's *me* who's jealous. I think I
courted the wrong girl — waddaya think — eh? (*Said lightly but with
a lot of truth in it*)
Brenda I think you don't change. That's what I think, Mickey. (*She
smiles*)

… and Ray, wearing the sweater, comes in from the terrace

Ray There you are, sweetheart.
Brenda We were just coming out
Ray Too late, they're all finished.

This as Polly and Francine come in

Francine Polly's just going.
Michael I'll drive you.
Polly No, no, that's all right — I rather fancy a walk. Get some fresh
air.

Francine Anyway, you've had far too much to drink, darling.
Ray Before you go, Polly — all that other business — it was just — you know — old friends — letting off steam.
Polly Oh — right.
Michael We're all happy again. All made up. Right Raymond?
Ray Right.
Francine So you can — take your leave — in the knowledge that everything is as it should be.

She "smiles"

Polly I wonder if you could umm like do me a favour before I go?
Michael And what is that, Polly?
Polly I was wondering if I could have a photograph.
Michael Of us? Delighted.

Polly takes out her small camera as:

Brenda All of us?
Ray Why not, sweetheart?
Francine Why not indeed.
Polly If I could have like Michael and Raymond in the middle ...

Ad lib as they take their places ... the two men in the middle, the two women next to their husbands, but:

(*Looking through the lens*) That's great.
Michael Actually ... we should have a glass in our hands. (*And he goes to collect glasses*)
Francine Sorry about this, Polly.

The following as Michael distributes wine glasses

Brenda Tell you what, Francine ... how near are we to Gibraltar?
Francine Oh ... couple of hours perhaps.
Ray Gibraltar?
Brenda I quite fancy having a look at it.
Michael As it happens I gotta go down there on a bitta business — we can make a day of it.
Brenda If it's not too much trouble.
Michael Leave it out, Bren — what are friends for?

By now they are back in line

All right Polly?

Polly Great.
Michael Tell you what though — let's change places — a bit of the old
  wife swopping eh Raymondo?

*More ad-libbing as places are changed, Francine standing next to Ray,
and Brenda next to Michael*

Michael (*raising his glass*) To trust ... respect ... and friendship.
Ray (*returning the toast*) Friendship.
Francine ⎱
Brenda ⎰ (*together; a little less enthusiastically*) Friendship.

*As Polly takes her photograph of them raising their glasses at the
camera:*

*The Lights change, and they freeze as a mirror image of them appears
on the screen ... and:*

CURTAIN

FURNITURE AND PROPERTY LIST

ACT I

On stage: Bar with glasses, beer, water, whisky, wine
Large flatscreen TV (operational) with DVD machine
Reclining swivel chair with matching footstool. *On footstool*: TV remote control
Other chairs, tables etc.
Cupboard containing safe
Telephone
Telephone directory
Intercom telephone
Collection of family photographs
Small pad of paper and pen
Silver-framed photograph for **Ray**
Glass of beer for **Michael**

Off stage: Rucksack containing document, tape recorder, mobile phone (**Polly**)
Small tray holding open bottle of white wine, wine glass, bowl of nuts, bowl of olives, napkins, bottles of beer, bottle opener (**Michael**)

Personal: **Ray**: packet of cigarettes, folded euros
Brenda: small bag

ACT II

Set: Dining table (with remains of informal barbecue meal, and low-burning candles) and chairs on terrace
Glass of water for **Ray**
In safe: handgun
In DVD machine: disc
*In **Polly**'s rucksack*: disc, small camera

Re-set: **Polly**'s rucksack propped against a chair

Off stage: Barbecue tongs, glass of whisky (**Michael**)
Drinks glasses (**Francine** and **Polly**)
Bottle of pills (**Brenda**)
Marigold gloves (**Francine**)

Tray with two mugs of coffee; one of tea with teabag; milk in jug, sugar in bowl (**Francine**)
Ray's sweater (**Brenda**)

Personal: **Michael**: keys
                 Brenda: handkerchief

LIGHTING PLOT

Practical fittings required: garden lights in Act II
One interior with exterior backing

ACT I

To open: General interior and exterior early afternoon lighting

No cues

ACT II

To open: General interior lighting; darkness on exterior with garden lights
effect

No cues

EFFECTS PLOT

ACT I

Cue 1   **Michael**: " … he swims like fucking Jaws."   (Page 5)
          Electronic buzzer

Cue 2   **Michael**: " … out on the golf course."   (Page 20)
          Door buzzer

Cue 3   **Michael**: "It's another world."   (Page 28)
          Telephone

Cue 4   **Michael**: " … would you reckon? Eh? Eh?"   (Page 33)
          Polly's *mobile phone rings*

Cue 5   **Michael**: "... I promise you." (He smiles)   (Page 34)
          Telephone

ACT II

Cue 6   **Ray**: " … I must say."   (Page 44)
          Electronic buzzer

Cue 7   **Brenda**: "Just the one?"   (Page 47)
          Electronic buzzer

Cue 8   **Brenda**: "That's just asking for …"   (Page 48)
          Gunshot

Cue 9   **Ray**: "Jesus Christ!"   (Page 48)
          Gunshot

Cue 10   **Michael**: "Good. Good to be of service."   (Page 52)
          Distant sound of fireworks

Cue 11   **Michael**: "And happy to oblige."   (Page 54)
          Distant fireworks

Cue 12   **Ray** moves away . Pause   (Page 65)
          Distant, bigger fireworks, and people cheering

Cue 13   **Brenda** shivers and pulls her cardigan closer   (Page 75)
          Fireworks and cheering

PROJECTION/VIDEO PLOT

ACT I